VENICE
AND ITS
MERCHANT EMPIRE

To Jenny

*G*rateful acknowledgment is made to Tracy Ehrlich
of the Department of Art/Art History at
Colgate University, Hamilton, New York,
for her generous assistance in reading the manuscript.

The author also wishes to thank the following scholars for so generously answering questions, giving advice, recommending resources, and offering other assistance: James S. Grubb, Margaret L. King, Albert Rabil, Thomas G. Olsen, Luci Fortunato De Lisle, Ann Rosalind Jones, Carol Harding, Mark D. Lew, Katherine McGinnis, Alexander Cowan, Anne J. Schutte, Chris Hermansen, Sheila Ffolliot, Sharon Farmer, Christopher Corley, Dan Price, Valery Rees, and Monica Chojnacka.

CULTURES
OF THE PAST

VENICE
AND ITS
MERCHANT EMPIRE

KATHRYN HINDS

BENCHMARK BOOKS

MARSHALL CAVENDISH

NEW YORK

Benchmark Books
Marshall Cavendish Corporation
99 White Plains Road
Tarrytown, New York 10591-9001

Website: www.marshallcavendish.com

Library of Congress Cataloging-in-Publication Data
Hinds, Kathryn, 1962–
    Venice and its merchant empire / Kathryn Hinds.
      p. cm. — (Cultures of the past)
    Includes bibliographical references and index.
    Summary: Examines the history, culture, religion, society, and achievements of the Italian city of Venice, from its founding to its surrender to Napoleon at the end of the eighteenth century.
    ISBN 0-7614-0305-1
    1. Venice (Italy)—History—Juvenile literature. [1. Venice (Italy)—History.]
I. Title. II. Series.
DG676 .H54   2001
945'.31—dc21   97-050353

Printed in Hong Kong

1 3 5 6 4 2

Book design by Carol Matsuyama
Photo research by Linda Sykes, Hilton Head, SC

Front cover: A view of the Rialto Bridge and the Grand Canal, painted in the nineteenth century by Samuel Prout

Back cover: A portrait of a Venetian woman and child by Paolo Veronese (1528–1588)

Photo Credits
Front cover, pages 25, 61: Christie's Images; back cover, pages 32, 41: Louvre/ Superstock; pages 6–7: Provost and Fellows of Eton College, Windsor/The Bridgeman Art Library International Ltd; pages 9,13, 72: Correr Museum, Venice/The Art Archive, London; page 11: Palazzo Pubblico, Siena, Italy/The Art Archive, London; page 12: Palazzo Ducale, Venice, Italy/Erich Lessing/Art Resource; page 17: Cassa di Risparmio della Marca Trevigiana, Treviso, Italy/AKG London; pages 18–19, 67: AKG London; page 21: Christie's Images/The Bridgeman Art Library International Ltd; pages 22, 47: Louvre/ Erich Lessing/ Art Resource; page 23: Galleria Nazionale d'Arte Antica, Rome, Italy/ Cameraphoto/ Art Resource; pages 24, 26: The Art Archive, London; page 28: Museo Vetrario, Murano/The Bridgeman Art Library International Ltd; page 29: Galleria dell' Accademia, Venice/ Erich Lessing/Art Resource; page 30: Staatliche Museen, Berlin, Germany/ Erich Lessing/Art Resource; page 33: Museum Bonnat, Bayonne /The Art Archive, London; pages 35, 65, 70: Superstock; page 38: Christie's/AKG London; pages 39, 49: Galleria dell' Accademia, Venice/The Bridgeman Art Library International Ltd; page 43: San Marco, Venice/The Bridgeman Art Library International Ltd; page 45: National Gallery, London/The Bridgeman Art Library International Ltd; page 50: Museo Correr, Venice/The Bridgeman Art Library International Ltd; page 52: Correr Museum, Venice/Superstock; pages 58–59: Coll. Crespi, Milan, Italy/Scala/Art Resource; page 63: Querini Stampalia Fd. /The Art Archive, London; page 69: Ca'Rezzonico Museo del Settecento Veneziano, Venice/Erich Lessing/Art Resource

CONTENTS

CHAPTER ONE

A REPUBLIC OF MERCHANTS AND SEAMEN

The city of Venice sits off the northeastern coast of Italy on a cluster of islands at the head of the Adriatic Sea. Today Venice is often thought of as just an especially beautiful place for a vacation. At one time, though, the Venetians were among the most powerful people in Europe. For a thousand years their city flourished as an independent state, the Most Serene Republic of Venice.

Humble Beginnings

The founders of Venice were citizens of the Roman Empire, which stretched from Britain to Asia Minor. In 364 C.E.* the empire was divided into two halves, the Western Empire and the Eastern, or Byzantine, Empire. The Adriatic Sea was the approximate boundary between them. In the fifth and sixth centuries the Western Empire fell apart as it was over-run by invaders. Many Roman citizens in northeastern Italy fled to the islands of the Venetian lagoon, the shallow body of water that connects to the head of the Adriatic.

*Many systems of dating have been used by different cultures throughout history. This series of books uses B.C.E. (Before Common Era) and C.E. (Common Era) instead of B.C. (Before Christ) and A.D. (Anno Domini) out of respect for the diversity of the world's peoples.

The islands were protected from invasion by treacherous marshes, sandbars, and winding channels. In this safe environment communities soon grew up. The islanders became expert sailors, fishers, and merchants. The lagoon supplied them not only with fish but also with sea salt. They were able to make a good living trading salt and salted fish up and down the Adriatic coast and along the rivers of eastern Italy.

Twelve townships formed on the lagoon islands. In 697 these townships decided to join together under one leader, called the doge, who was elected by an assembly of the people. The Republic of Venice was born.

Venice around the year 1600. The city's watery location helped make it "The Queen of the Seas."

A Growing Sea Power

By the tenth century Venetian merchants had extended their business to the eastern shores of the Mediterranean Sea. There they traded with the Byzantine Empire and the Muslim states of the Near East. But Slavic pirates on the Adriatic continually threatened the city's trade routes. So in the year 1000 Doge Pietro Orseolo II led a fleet to attack the pirate bases on the coast of Dalmatia (modern Croatia). His success was complete. Venice gained control of the Adriatic and also brought Dalmatia under its rule.

Meanwhile the once mighty Byzantine Empire was weakening. In 1081 the emperor sought Venice's help against Norman forces, from northern France, who were conquering the empire's possessions in southern Italy. The Venetians were able to slow the Norman advance. In gratitude, the emperor gave them the right to trade at many Byzantine ports without paying the usual fees. He also awarded Venetian merchants their own quarter in Constantinople (now Istanbul, Turkey), the Byzantine capital.

The First Crusade

The year 1095 saw the beginning of the First Crusade, when the Christians of Europe set out to conquer Palestine, the Holy Land of Jews, Muslims, and Christians. This region on the eastern coast of the Mediterranean had been under Muslim rule for four centuries. Although the Venetian republic was devoutly Christian, it was reluctant to disrupt its trade with the Muslim world. So at first Venice stayed out of the crusade.

In 1099 the crusaders captured Jerusalem, Palestine's most important city, and set up several kingdoms in the region. The Italian city-states of Pisa and Genoa, which had taken part in the crusade, now extended their trade routes into the eastern Mediterranean. This was a great threat to Venetian power. When the crusader leader asked Venice for ships and supplies, the republic could not afford to refuse.

On the way to Palestine, Venice's fleet fought and defeated a fleet from Pisa, forcing the Pisans out of the eastern Mediterranean for good. In Palestine the Venetians helped the crusaders take the city of Haifa. In return for its help Venice received many privileges, including free trading rights throughout the crusaders' domains, a third of Haifa, and all of the Lebanese city of Tripoli, a key seaport. The republic's position in the Eastern markets was now secure.

Venetian warships battle a fleet from Genoa. The ships' sails are furled, giving the rowers the full advantages of speed and maneuverability.

WARFARE ON THE WAVES

The Venetians owed their supremacy on the Adriatic and Mediterranean Seas not only to their skill at trade but also to their skill at naval warfare. In time of need, almost any Venetian ship could become a warship, any sailor a fighter. But for centuries the Venetian war galley, with its sleek design and highly trained crew, was the republic's most reliable weapon.

Before gunpowder came into common use in the 1400s, sea battles were fought almost just as they had been in ancient times. As a war galley closed in on an enemy ship, archers fired volleys of arrows across the water. With the oarsmen rowing at top speed, the galley tried to ram into and sink the enemy. At other times the war galley would maneuver alongside the enemy ship so that soldiers could leap aboard it. Bloody sword fights and hand-to-hand combat would follow, until the boarding party either took over the ship or was beaten off. This shipboard fighting was usually what decided who won the battle.

When ships were attacking a port city, they used catapults to hurl stones at the city's walls. The Venetians also made use of flying bridges. These were platforms that could be raised up a ship's mast. The platforms hung out in front of the ship, and soldiers charged across them to get to the top of the city walls.

From the late fifteenth century, Venetian soldier-sailors relied more and more on hand-held firearms. Sixteenth-century warfare saw the growing importance of cannon fire. Eventually Venetian warships carried as many as thirty cannons. This meant, however, that the Venetians had to come up with new ship designs and abandon the fast, maneuverable galleys that had first given them mastery of the seas.

Venice and Constantinople

The twelfth century was a time of upheaval in the relationship between Venice and the Byzantine Empire. The citizens of Constantinople increasingly resented the privileges granted to the city's Venetian merchants. Hostilities exploded in 1171, when the emperor ordered the arrest of all Venetians in the empire. Although the Venetians' rights were soon restored, hard feelings between the two powers remained.

These years also saw important increases in Venice's power. By the mid-twelfth century the republic controlled Istria, a peninsula on the northeastern Adriatic. In 1177 the doge hosted peace talks between the pope (the head of the Catholic Church) and the ruler of the Holy Roman Empire. This empire, trying to revive the might of ancient Rome, extended from Germany and Austria into northern Italy. Venice's role as mediator between pope and emperor put it on an equal footing with the two greatest powers in Europe.

The Fourth Crusade

In 1199 the pope urged Christians to begin a new crusade, the fourth. The crusaders planned on taking an army of 30,000 men to Palestine. Such a force could be transported only with help from Venice, the one European state with the resources to build a large enough fleet. The doge agreed to provide ships and men and also to feed the gigantic army for a year. In return the crusaders pledged to give Venice a huge amount of money and half of all territory conquered during the crusade.

In 1202 the crusaders gathered in Venice, but the leaders were unable to pay the republic all they had promised. The doge decided to allow them to pay the rest after they had plundered their enemies. The crusaders also had to agree to help reconquer Zara, a Dalmatian city that had rebelled against Venetian rule. At least two hundred ships set out, the doge himself sailing in the foremost vessel.

Zara was soon retaken. While the conquerors wintered in Dalmatia, an exiled Byzantine prince persuaded them to go next to Constantinople. The crusaders and Venetians attacked the Byzantine capital in 1203, then followed with a far more brutal attack in April 1204. They killed men, women, and children in huge numbers. They spent three days looting Constantinople, helping themselves to all the valuables they could carry off. The crusaders could finally pay the Venetians what

Pope Alexander III gives a spear to Doge Ziani, asking for the Venetian leader's help in a dispute with the Holy Roman Emperor.

they owed them. They never did go to Palestine.

Venice came away from the Fourth Crusade with more than money and plunder. In the division of Byzantine territory, the Venetians received three eighths of Constantinople, the western coast of Greece, and a large number of islands in the Aegean Sea, including Crete. The little republic had become an empire.

Venetians and crusaders storm the walls of Constantinople. Although most people today are horrified by the violence of the Fourth Crusade, the conquest of Constantinople did cement Venice's role as a world power.

Focus on Italy

The Venetians acquired territory mainly to make sure they had the best conditions for trade. Coastal and island colonies gave them secure bases for protecting their shipping routes. Increasingly, Venice also wished to dominate the rivers and roadways that led to Europe's inland markets. In 1240 the republic concluded a treaty that gave it command of the Po River, the most important waterway connecting the Adriatic to the interior of northern Italy. Now all merchandise bound for that region had to pass through the port of Venice.

Venice's ever-increasing power did not go unchallenged. The city-state of Genoa, on Italy's northwestern coast, was a fierce rival for command of the Mediterranean trade routes. In 1257 Venice and Genoa went to war. It took more than a hundred years and three additional wars for Venice to put an end to Genoa's threat to its superiority.

There were other troubles besides the wars with Genoa. In 1310 three Venetian nobles attempted to overthrow the government. In 1347 plague killed three-fifths of the city's people. Eight years later, the doge tried to make himself a dictator—and was beheaded for it.

GOVERNING THE REPUBLIC

The government of the Most Serene Republic of Venice was unlike that of any other European state of the Middle Ages or Renaissance. It evolved slowly over many centuries, taking its final form in the year 1310.

The doge was the head of state. His actual powers were quite limited, but as the living symbol of the republic, he had great influence. His presence was required at every meeting of every branch of the government. Six councillors both assisted him and made certain he did not try to increase his authority. These councillors were elected three at a time and stayed in office for only eight months.

The republic's laws were made by the Senate, which also dealt with such issues as foreign affairs, finances, trade policies, and care of the lagoon. The Senate was a body of 120 men elected for one-year terms. It also included as many as 155 other officials. Senators and most other officeholders were elected by the Great Council, which was made up of all Venetian noblemen aged twenty-five and above. The Great Council's approval was required for all of the Senate's decisions.

The members of the Great Council were under constant scrutiny by the Council of Ten. The ten councillors, elected for one-year terms, saw that swift and ruthless punishment was dealt to any noble who abused his position, conspired to overthrow Venice's government, or plotted with foreign powers.

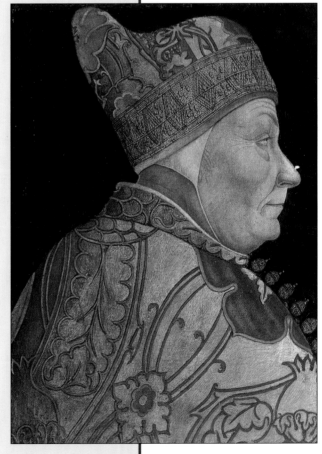

As the living symbol of Venice, the doge wore elaborate ceremonial clothing to show off the republic's wealth and grandeur. In this portrait, painted around 1460, Doge Francesco Foscari is dressed in a gorgeous silk brocade robe and matching corno, *a special hat that only the doge and his wife were allowed to wear.*

The republic not only survived these and other trials but emerged from them stronger than ever. By 1450 Venice had conquered more than half of northern Italy. Venice also ruled the Greek island of Corfu, a major base in the southern Adriatic. In 1473 the republic gained control of the large Mediterranean island of Cyprus. As Pope Pius II had commented not long before, the Venetians were now "the most powerful people on both land and sea."

Enemies on All Sides

Even as Venice's power peaked, a new enemy was rising in the East. In 1453 the Ottoman Turks, rulers of an empire based in Asia Minor, conquered Constantinople. Soon they possessed most of the Balkan Peninsula. In 1499 the Turks defeated Venice in a disastrous naval battle. The republic was forced to surrender several of its Greek bases.

Nevertheless, Venice's ambitions continued to grow. By the early 1500s the republic ruled much of the Papal States, an area of north-central Italy that had long been controlled by the pope. As a result, Pope Julius II, France, Spain, and the Holy Roman Empire formed the League of Cambrai in 1508, and their forces marched toward Venice.

Venice fought alone against this alliance, suffering some terrible losses. After two years the League of Cambrai began to fall apart. The pope, satisfied with regaining the Papal States, made peace with Venice. Through determination, sacrifice, and skillful diplomacy the republic held out as other alliances shifted. By 1517 Venice had recovered most of its lost territories.

During the next fifty years France, Spain, and the Holy Roman Empire continued to battle for control of the Italian peninsula. Venice played a balancing act, leaning sometimes toward France and sometimes toward Spain. The city in the lagoon was never attacked, and the people of Venice's mainland territories remained loyal to the republic throughout the conflicts. Venice was one of the few Italian states to come out of the wars independent and whole.

Battling the Turks

During the Italian wars the Ottoman Empire continued to expand, becoming a serious threat to all of Europe. In 1538 Venice joined the pope and

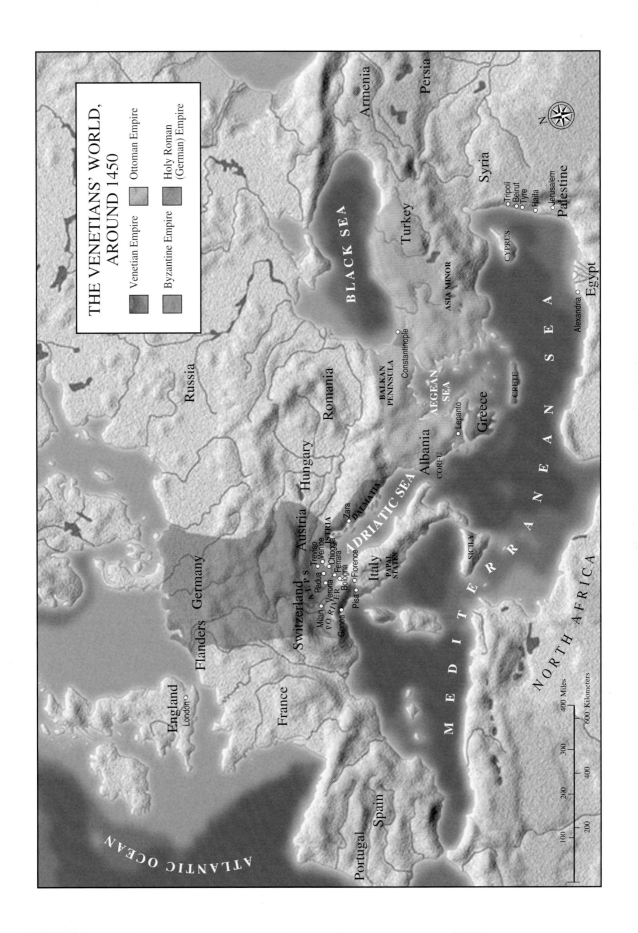

THE VENETIANS' WORLD,
AROUND 1450

Venetian Empire

Byzantine Empire

Ottoman Empire

Holy Roman
(German) Empire

N

ATLANTIC OCEAN

England
London

Flanders

Germany

France

Switzerland

Austria

Hungary

Russia

Romania

BLACK SEA

Armenia

Persia

Turkey

Syria

Tripoli
Beirut
Tyre
Haifa
Jerusalem
Palestine

CYPRUS

ASIA MINOR

Constantinople

BALKAN
PENINSULA

AEGEAN
SEA

Greece

CRETE

Lepanto

Albania

CORFU

Alexandria

Egypt

ALPS

Milan
PO RIVER
Genoa
Pisa

Treviso
Padua
Verona
Bologna

Venice
Chioggia
Ferrara
Florence

ISTRIA

Zara

DALMATIA

ADRIATIC SEA

Italy

PAPAL
STATES

SICILY

MEDITERRANEAN SEA

NORTH AFRICA

Portugal

Spain

400 Miles

600 Kilometers

100   200   300   400

200   400   600

the Holy Roman emperor in a league against the Turks. The allies lost a decisive naval battle, and with it Venice permanently lost its supremacy on the sea.

In 1571 Venice, Pope Pius V, and the king of Spain made another alliance to fight the Ottomans. The Holy League, as it was called, assembled a mighty 208-ship fleet, to which Venice contributed 110 warships. The fleet met the Turkish navy in the Gulf of Lepanto off the western coast of Greece. The battle was ferocious, but at the end of the day the Ottoman force was utterly destroyed. The Holy League's victory was celebrated all over Europe.

As glorious as the triumph at Lepanto was, it had little practical effect. Venice had already lost Cyprus to the Turks, and within a year the Ottoman navy was rebuilt.

The End of an Era

As a great power, Venice was in decline. The battles with the Turks had severely strained the republic's resources. Also, the discovery of new sea routes by Christopher Columbus and other explorers had brought major changes to the world of trade. Merchant ships could now sail around Africa or even cross the Atlantic Ocean to new sources of wealth. England, the Netherlands, France, and Spain had the easiest access to the new shipping routes and became Europe's great powers. The Venetians began to turn from trade to investing in land and agriculture on the Italian mainland.

One last attempt to recapture Venice's past glory came in 1684, when Venetian general Francesco Morosini won Greece's southern peninsula from the Turks. But the republic held this territory for just thirty years, and then lost it again to Ottoman forces. Venice's only overseas possessions now were the Dalmatian coastland and the islands off western Greece.

No longer an essential link in East-West trade, Venice took on a new role. In the seventeenth and eighteenth centuries it became the playgound of Europe. Wealthy people from all over the continent came to the beautiful city to enjoy its festivals, theaters, concerts, and gambling houses. Venice became renowned as one of the most cultured and pleasure-filled cities in the world.

Napoleon (standing in front of the mirror) presents his demands to representatives of the Venetian people.

And so it was when Napoleon Bonaparte of France led his army into Italy. Napoleon reached the edge of the lagoon and declared war on Venice on May 1, 1797. On the twelfth, the doge and the ruling nobles stepped down and turned the government over to the people. The city surrendered to Napoleon, ending more than a thousand years of independence.

CHAPTER TWO

THE JEWEL OF THE ADRIATIC

In 1581 Francesco Sansovino described his hometown in a book called *Venice, Most Noble and Singular City*. This title expressed the character of Venice well. The republic had an extraordinarily rich and unique culture, made possible by the Venetians' mastery of the sea.

The Queen of Cities

Venice had a style all its own, combining influences from both western Europe and the East. Rows of pointed arches, fancifully shaped chimneys, rooftop balconies, and domed churches all gave the city a distinctive look. And unlike other European cities, Venice had no walls or fortifications of any kind—the Venetians trusted to the surrounding lagoon to protect them.

This seventeenth-century painting shows a favorite view of Venice. On the left are the Zecca, or mint, and the Library of Saint Mark. Behind them rises the Campanile, Venice's famous bell tower. On the right is the Doge's Palace, in back of which can be seen the dome of the Basilica of Saint Mark. In front of the Doge's Palace the lavish state galley is about to set out into the lagoon, accompanied by other boats. The small boats that are propelled with poles by one or two standing men are gondolas, vessels unique to Venice.

Venice was built upon a large number of islands with a maze of canals running between them. Each island, according to Sansovino, had a well in the middle of a public square, several churches, and all the businesses that people needed on a daily basis. Streets or footpaths ran alongside the canals, which could be crossed by bridges. People also traveled from place to place by boat, so each canal had many boat landings.

Buildings were constructed on stone foundations laid over dense fields of long wooden poles sunk into the sandy lagoon bottom. Most houses and churches were built from brick. The outside walls might be painted or plastered, and many were faced with a fine white limestone imported from Istria. Paintings, coats of arms, and sculptures of saints decorated many building fronts.

The Heart of Venice

The main route through Venice was the Grand Canal—"the most beautiful street . . . in the whole world," according to a French historian writing in

AT HOME IN VENICE

Venice has always been well known for its beautiful palaces— in 581 Francesco Sansovino counted more than one hundred, noting that other cities had only five or six. The Venetian palace developed during the Middle Ages, when it functioned as a wealthy merchant's home and place of business.

The palace was usually three stories tall, with each floor divided into a large middle section and a smaller section on each side. The first level was given over to business. The front entrance, facing the water, had a quay or dock. The central doorway led into a spacious hall where goods could be unloaded and inventoried. On either side of the entrance hall, and half its height, were storerooms. The merchant had his offices on a mezzanine level above the storerooms.

The central section of the second floor was called the *sala*. This was often used as a showroom for merchandise. It was also the place where banquets, weddings, and other gatherings were held. The *sala* traditionally had a row of high windows across the front. To the sides of the *sala* were the family's living quarters. The top floor provided rooms for servants and employees.

By the Renaissance most Venetians were renters rather than home owners. A wealthy Venetian might rent part of a palace or a suite of rooms in a luxury apartment building. There were also apartment buildings for middle- and lower-income families, and even rent-free apartments for the very poor.

1494. At about the midpoint of the Grand Canal was the Rialto (ree-AHL-toh), the business quarter of the city. This was also the location of the only bridge over the Grand Canal.

Near the southeastern end of the Grand Canal was the heart of the city, Saint Mark's Square. Here Venetians gathered for all solemn and festive occasions. Even on ordinary days the square was filled with people doing business and socializing.

The square was dominated by the Basilica of Saint Mark. This splendid domed church was modeled on a church in Constantinople. Byzantine artists were hired to decorate the basilica with Greek-style mosaics. Over the years many treasures from the East were brought to adorn Saint Mark's, including a great amount of plunder from the Fourth Crusade.

Next to the basilica was the Doge's Palace, the power center of the republic. All of the councils that took part in governing Venice met here, and so did all the courts. The most important room in the Doge's Palace was the Hall of the Great Council. This was where the nobles of Venice—as many as two thousand men—gathered to elect the republic's officials and ratify legislation. The

In Rialto Square, merchants gather to socialize and do business, while a couple of women make their way through the crowd to go to the church on the left. In the buildings at the center and right, bankers have their counters set up under the arches. This scene was painted by Luca Carlevaris in the early eighteenth century.

In the Hall of the Great Council, the doge (on a raised platform at the back) addresses Venice's noblemen. This painting by Francesco Guardi (an eighteenth-century artist who lived in Venice all his life) captures the grandeur of the immense room, with its ornately carved ceiling and huge wall and ceiling paintings.

walls and ceiling were painted with religious and historical scenes by the finest artists in the city.

Across a narrow plaza from the Doge's Palace were the Zecca and the Library of Saint Mark, both designed by the great sixteenth-century architect Jacopo Sansovino. The Zecca housed the mint, where the republic's coins were produced. The library was one of the finest in Europe and held an impressive collection of manuscripts, books, and maps.

Sansovino was one of several prominent architects working in Venice during the sixteenth and seventeenth centuries. Others included Vincenzo Scamozzi, Michele Sanmicheli, and Baldassare Longhena. These men contributed many beautiful public buildings, churches, and palaces to the city. Most notable of all was Andrea Palladio. His masterpieces were the Venetian churches of San Giorgio Maggiore, Il Redentore, and Santa Maria della Presentazione. He also designed a number of beautiful villas, or

Two centuries after Palladio's lifetime, the Venetian artist Canaletto put together three of the great architect's designs in this fantasy image of Venice. The painting combines Palladio's never-used plan for a bridge over the Grand Canal with a palace (left) and church (right) that he designed for another Italian city.

country houses, in Venice's mainland territories. Palladio's exquisite buildings, together with his writings on architecture, made him Europe's most influential architect for centuries.

Ships of State

On the eastern edge of Venice was the Arsenal, where the state's merchant ships and warships were built. At its height the Arsenal was Europe's largest manufacturing center, employing about two thousand workers. More than a hundred ships might be under construction at the same time, sheltered in long brick sheds. The whole complex was surrounded by a high, windowless wall, which sentries patrolled constantly. For security reasons, the Arsenal had only one doorway, and the sea gate was large enough for just one ship to pass through at a time.

Specialized craftsmen made not only the ships themselves

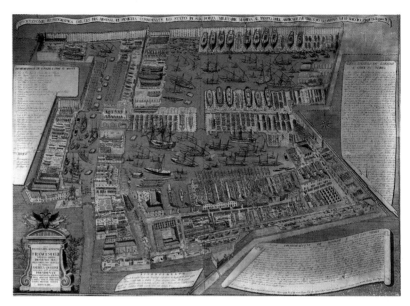

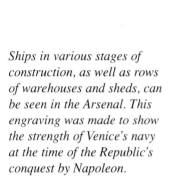

Ships in various stages of construction, as well as rows of warehouses and sheds, can be seen in the Arsenal. This engraving was made to show the strength of Venice's navy at the time of the Republic's conquest by Napoleon.

but also everything necessary to fit them out, including oars, rowing benches, ropes, and sails. When a ship was ready to be launched, it was towed down the long canal leading to the sea gate. On either side of this canal were warehouses. The various fittings, along with weapons and provisions, were handed out the warehouse windows to be installed. This system was so efficient that ten ships could be completely fitted out and put to sea within six hours.

The first ships built in the Arsenal were galleys—long, sleek vessels that could move swiftly under either oar or sail power. Galleys made formidable warships. Cargo ships, called cogs, were built at private shipyards located throughout the city. These sailing ships were bulky and slow, but also wonderfully durable.

In the late 1200s features of the galley and the cog were combined to make a new type of vessel, the great galley. This was a long ship that was wider and deeper than the older galley. It was so fast that it could sail from Italy to England in just a month. Great galleys were owned and operated by the Venetian state. Each vessel had a crew of 180 oarsmen and 20 to 30 archers (or, later, gunners). These ships were entrusted with the most precious cargoes and frequently served as warships.

By the 1450s the cog had developed into the carrack, a more maneuverable, tougher vessel that was able to sail even in the stormy winter months. Armed with tiers of cannon, carracks grew so formidable that they were eventually enlisted to carry luxury goods overseas. Most Venetian merchant ships, however, remained smaller vessels that engaged in local trade around the Adriatic.

The Lifeblood of the Republic

Venice grew beautiful, wealthy, and powerful because of its total devotion to trade. Most of the republic's officials were either merchants or ex-merchants, so government policies were always favorable to trade. Ships loaded and unloaded not only on the Grand Canal but on smaller canals throughout the city. There were warehouses full of imports in every district. On the Rialto bankers made financial arrangements not only with local merchants, but also with traders from Europe and the East.

The Grand Canal was a lively place, with warehouses full of imported goods and merchants plying their trade. This scene was painted in the 1800s and shows the famous Rialto Bridge in the background.

Venetian merchants traveled extensively, often spending years in foreign lands. They could be found in trading centers from London to Constantinople. Some voyaged even farther. The most famous Venetian merchant-traveler was Marco Polo. He wrote about his adventures in a book he called *The Description of the World* (now usually known as *The Travels of Marco Polo*).

According to his book, Marco Polo left Venice in 1271, when he was seventeen, to go to China with his father and uncle. A difficult four-year journey finally brought the Polos to the court of China's emperor, Kublai Khan. The emperor took the young Venetian into his service, sending him on numerous diplomatic missions. Marco traveled all over China and also to India, Tibet, and Southeast Asia. Everywhere he went, he carefully observed and remembered scenery, customs, and, especially, details of local trade.

At length the Polos grew homesick, and in 1292 they set out for Venice. On their arrival they were greeted with astonishment. The tales they told of their travels and their long stay in the East were incredible. And the rich robes and fabulous jewels they brought back made a deep impression on their fellow Venetians. By 1325 there was a sizable Venetian community in Zaitun, a Chinese port city.

As for Marco, three years after returning to Venice, he had a professional writer help him compose *The Description of the World.* Some modern historians doubt Marco Polo's story, which certainly contains some exaggerations and also leaves out descriptions of many common Chinese

Marco Polo's Description of the World *was so popular that it was one of the earliest books to be published after the invention of the printing press. This illustration of the famous merchant-traveler appeared in the first printed edition of Marco's book, in 1477.*

customs. These historians feel that if Marco Polo had really been to China, he would have written about such things. But Marco himself said at the time of his death, "I did not write half of what I saw." In any case, whether or not *The Description of the World* was completely true, it was a medieval and Renaissance best-seller. Not only did it inspire the explorations of Christopher Columbus and others, but it also gave generations of Europeans a rare glimpse of life in faraway places.

And it was not only wealthy merchants who participated in trade. Both large and small shares in merchant voyages were sold to investors. Almost any Venetian, at any level of society, could take part in the city's most vital activity. Doges, bishops, widows, craftspeople, and common sailors all invested in and profited from trade.

The Seven Great Convoys

During the golden age of Venetian trade, from the 1330s to the 1530s, the state organized its great galleys into regular convoys that traveled to the major overseas trading posts. Only Venetian citizens could consign merchandise to be carried on these convoys, which were called *mudas* (MOO-dahs).

Seven *mudas* sailed from Venice every year. Their destinations were Alexandria, Egypt; Syria and Palestine; northwestern Africa and Spain; Sicily and North Africa; Constantinople and the Black Sea; southern France; and England and Flanders. Some of these *mudas* also called at Crete, Cyprus, and other Mediterranean ports. At every stop the convoys loaded precious goods: spices, perfumes, medicines, dyes, silk, linen, fine wool, cloth, wine, raisins, sugar, gold, ivory, amber, and furs. Much of this merchandise originally came from as far away as Russia, China, India, and southern Africa.

When the *mudas* returned home, some of their cargo went into the city's shops. Some was bought in bulk by merchants from other nations, who came to Venice knowing they could find or order goods of all kinds. Much of the merchandise was warehoused while arrangements were made on the Rialto to ship it elsewhere.

The great galleys that sailed in the *mudas* made up a very small part of Venice's total merchant fleet. In 1423 these ships numbered only twenty-five out of more than three thousand vessels. Most Venetian merchant ships carried less spectacular cargo than that found on the convoys, such as wood, metals, hemp, grain, salt, stone, honey, beeswax, olive oil, and cotton.

Luxury Exports

Venice was an important manufacturing center and exported many of its products. The processing of salt, sugar, and wax supplied the needs of

This pitcher in the form of a ship is an example of the luxurious glassware produced in Venice during the Renaissance. It was probably made by Ermonia Vivarini, a woman from a noted family of artists and glassmakers, around the year 1520.

both Venetians and their trading partners. More luxurious products included soap, perfume, jewelry, and lace.

The republic's most prestigious industry was glass manufacturing. Venetian glassmakers crafted elegant goblets, pitchers, and bowls in clear, colored, multicolored, and "lacy" glass. They also made mirrors, prized all over Europe, and window-panes. Other Venetian craftspeople used glass bars to create beautiful beads. For several hundred years Venice was a center for the manu-facturing of elegant pottery, too.

From the fourteenth through sixteenth centuries Venice was one of Europe's greatest silk manufactur-ing centers. Artisans spun and dyed imported raw silk and wove it into taffetas, velvets, and other luxury fabrics. Later the city also produced and exported exceptionally fine woolen cloth.

Masters of Light and Color

Toward the end of the fifteenth century Venice entered its great-est artistic period. Architecture and painting flourished as never before. Splendid new government buildings, palaces, churches, and meeting halls sprang up throughout the city. Everywhere, in new buildings and old, walls and ceilings were adorned with opu-lent paintings.

Two brothers, Gentile (jen-TEE-lay) and Giovanni (joh-VAH-nee) Bellini, founded a specifically Venetian style of painting, which emphasized the elements of light and color. Giovanni Bellini was credited with making it fashionable for illustrious Venetians to have their portraits painted. He also produced striking religious paintings. Both brothers painted many scenes from Venetian history. The Bellinis strongly influenced a number of younger Venetian artists, including Vittore Carpaccio (kar-PAH-chee-oh), Lorenzo Lotto, and Giorgione (jor-JOH-nay).

One of Gentile Bellini's most famous paintings, the Miracle of the Holy Cross *is a fairly accurate portrait of a Venice neighborhood at the end of the fifteenth century. The painting illustrates a story that was well known to Venetians of the time: while crossing a bridge in a procession, a group of monks accidentally dropped a golden cross into the canal below. This object contained a bit of wood that was said to be a piece of the cross on which Jesus died. Several people jumped into the canal to try to recover it, and one monk was successful. He swims at the front, holding up the precious religious object while onlookers kneel in prayer.*

The most gifted of Giovanni Bellini's students was Titian (TISH-uhn), regarded today as one of Europe's greatest artists. Titian's early works closely resembled those of Bellini. The paintings of his middle years showed a love of rich textures and had a strong sense of physical reality. His later art was characterized by softened shapes, glimmering lights, and a feeling of power. Throughout his lengthy career, Titian was a supreme master of the use of color.

The most important Venetian painters to follow Titian were Tintoretto and Paolo Veronese. Both these men were employed by the state to redecorate the walls and ceilings of the Doge's Palace after a disastrous

Titian painted this portrait of himself in 1562. The dramatic use of light and the feeling of intensity are typical of the paintings he made toward the end of his life.

fire in 1577. Tintoretto was also noted for his superb portraits, as was his daughter and apprentice, Marietta. Venice's last major artist was the eighteenth-century master Giambattista Tiepolo (tee-AY-poh-loh), whose frescoes and ceiling paintings adorned many Venetian churches and palaces.

Great Performances

During the Renaissance, Venice became a great musical center. Adrian Willaert (WILL-ert), music director of Saint Mark's, and Andrea Gabrieli, an organist at the basilica, were largely responsible for the development of the madrigal. This was a song, for four to six singers, in which each singer's line was an independent melody. Madrigals were sung by professional performers as well as by upper-class people who sang together for their own enjoyment.

Andrea Gabrieli's nephew Giovanni Gabrieli also became an organist at Saint Mark's, as well as a brilliant composer. His greatest pieces were written specifically for performance in the basilica. Many used two choirs, each singing from a different balcony. Sometimes Gabrieli added a small group of instruments and placed these in a third balcony. The choirs and instruments sang and played together in different combinations, wrapping Saint Mark's in blankets of beautiful sound.

Operas and Orchestras

The most important composer in seventeenth-century Venice was Claudio Monteverdi, music director of Saint Mark's for thirty years. Monteverdi wrote a great deal of church music as well as wonderful madrigals. But he is most famous as the world's first great opera composer. Monteverdi's masterpiece was *The Coronation of Poppea*, first performed in Venice in 1642. This opera told a dramatic story of love and revenge, set in ancient Rome. Monteverdi's music reflected all the characters' varied emotions. *Poppea* was a perfect blending of poetry, music, and spectacle. It helped make Venice the opera capital of Europe.

Many Venetians went to the opera or to one of the city's numerous concerts every night. During the eighteenth century, concerts featuring women singers and all-female orchestras were hosted by Venice's four *ospedali* (oh-speh-DAH-lee). These were orphanages that specialized in

A portrait of a woman, her son, and his dog by Paolo Veronese. Although Veronese is most famous today for his paintings of historical and mythological scenes, he had a great ability to communicate the moods and attitudes of the people in his portraits. He was especially skilled at portraying children realistically.

teaching girls to sing, compose, and play instruments. The orchestra of the Ospedale della Pietà was praised as one of the best in Europe.

The great Venetian composer Antonio Vivaldi was music director of the Ospedale della Pietà from 1704 to 1740. Many of Vivaldi's works were written specifically for the girls and women of that *ospedale*. He specialized in concertos, pieces in which an orchestra accompanies a solo instrument or a small group of instruments. Vivaldi's beautiful melodies are still well loved, and his concerto *The Four Seasons* is one of the most popular pieces of classical music today.

Comedy Tonight

Plays were another extremely popular form of entertainment in
eenth century saw the birth of the
-dee-uh- dell AR-tay) in Venice,
of theater used a cast of stereo-
d miser, a sassy maid, and young
and made up their lines as they
a great deal of clowning around
nally commedia dell'arte was per-
quares during festivals, but it came
mes and the theaters as well.

the playwright Carlo Goldoni took
arte and began to transform them
eaving behind masks and stereo-
people in real situations. He accu-
d the Venetian society of his time,
Venetians loved to see themselves
i's plays. As the German author
enice, "they shouted with laughter

A scene from the commedia dell'arte, portraying the characters without their masks. The old miser Pantalone (in red) scolds his daughter, Isabella, who has probably been spending time with a young man against her father's wishes. The other two characters in the scene are Pantalone's friend The Doctor (left) and Brighella, the old miser's scheming servant (right).

CHAPTER THREE

ALL FOR THE GRACE OF GOD

By the time of the First Crusade, in 1095, most Europeans, including most Venetians, were Christians. Then as now, Christianity was based on belief in one all-powerful, all-knowing God, present everywhere at every time. This article of faith was also held by Jews and Muslims. Christians were unique, however, in believing that the one God was revealed as three persons, distinct from one another yet completely unified. The three-in-one, or Trinity, was made up of God the Father, God the Son, and God the Holy Spirit. The Son was Jesus Christ, and his life and teachings were the centerpoint of Christianity.

The Story of Jesus

Jesus was a Jew who lived in Palestine from around 4 B.C.E. to 30 C.E. His story is told in the Gospels, the first four books of the New Testament of the Bible.

The Gospels relate that Jesus was the son of God, born as a human being in order to save humanity from its sins. His mother was Mary, the wife of a carpenter named Joseph. Before Jesus was born, the angel Gabriel visited Mary to tell her that she would become pregnant with a son who would be great and holy. (This event came to be known as the Annunciation.) When it was time for the birth, Mary and Joseph were away from home and had to take shelter in a stable. Angels appeared to shepherds nearby to tell them of the holy infant, and a bright star guided wise men from the East to the birthplace. Shepherds and wise men alike knelt to honor the newborn baby.

When Jesus was around thirty years old, he went to his cousin John for baptism. This was a ritual in which John symbolically cleansed people of their past sins so that they could begin to live more righteous lives. After Jesus was baptized, the Holy Spirit came down to him in the shape of a dove, and a heavenly voice proclaimed, "Thou art my beloved Son; with thee I am well pleased" (Luke 3:22).*

*All biblical quotations are from the Holy Bible, Revised Standard Version.

As a troop of Roman soldiers were leading Jesus to the place of his execution, "they compelled a passerby, Simon of Cyrene . . . to carry his cross." (Mark 15:21) This painting by Titian shows Simon taking the cross from Jesus' shoulders.

For the next three years Jesus traveled through Palestine, performing miracles, healing the sick, and teaching. Many of his lessons centered on the power of love—"You shall love your neighbor as yourself" (Matthew 22:39)—and the importance of the Golden Rule—"Whatever you wish that men would do to you, do so to them" (Matthew 7:12). He also taught that those who believed in him and followed his teachings would have an eternal life in the presence of God. Jesus attracted a large number of followers, both women and men. Twelve of these followers, men known as the disciples or apostles, were his most devoted students.

Some people feared that Jesus was trying to start a rebellion and would make himself king of the Jews, so he was arrested and put on trial. The Romans condemned him to death, and he was crucified, or executed by being hung on a cross. Three days later, the Bible says, some of his women followers went to his tomb and found it empty. An angel told them that Jesus had been resurrected—he had risen from the dead. After this Jesus appeared several times to his followers, promising forgiveness of sins and resurrection to all who believed in him.

Forty days after rising from the dead, Jesus ascended to heaven and rejoined God the Father. Ten days later the Holy Spirit came to the disciples and filled them with courage and inspiration. They began to spread Jesus' teachings and to preach that he was the savior of humankind. Through their efforts the Christian religion was founded.

The Church

For the first few centuries after Jesus' death, Christianity grew slowly. Then in 313 it became the official faith of the Roman Empire. After the fall of the Western Empire in the fifth century, the Christian Church continued to increase in power.

The Church was highly organized. Every town and village was made up of one or more parishes. Each parish had its own church and parish priest. A number of parishes were overseen by a high-ranking priest called a bishop. The most important bishops were the patriarch of Constantinople and the bishop of Rome, or pope.

The pope was regarded as the successor of Saint Peter, one of Jesus' disciples. The name *Peter* means "rock." Before Jesus died he had said to Peter, "On this rock I will build my church. . . . I will give you the keys of the kingdom of heaven" (Matthew 16:18–9). These statements were interpreted to give the pope a great deal of power.

The patriarch of Constantinople and the other Byzantine bishops were reluctant to accept the pope's authority. They had serious disagreements with some of the practices and beliefs of the western European churches. For example, in the Byzantine Empire married men could become priests, but in western Europe they could not. Gradually Byzantine Christianity and western European Christianity grew apart. In 1054 Christianity split into two factions, the Catholic Church in the West and the Orthodox Church in the East.

Venice, on the dividing line between West and East, held to the Catholic Church. Nevertheless, many of the city's religious practices continued to follow Eastern patterns. Churches were built and decorated in the Byzantine style. As in the East, families often used icons, special religious paintings, in their home worship.

I BELIEVE

In the fourth century, two Church councils issued a statement of Christianity's central beliefs. This became known as the Credo, from its first line in Latin, *Credo in unum Deum*—"I believe in one God." From 1014 on, every Catholic mass included the singing or reciting of the Credo. Here is an English translation of this declaration of faith:

I believe in one God, the Father almighty, maker of heaven and earth, and of all things visible and invisible. And in one Lord, Jesus Christ, only begotten son of God, born of his Father before all worlds. God from God, light from light, true God from true God; begotten, not made, being of one substance with the Father, through whom all things were made. Who for our salvation came down from heaven. And was made flesh by the Holy Spirit from within the Virgin Mary, and was made man. And for our sake he was crucified under Pontius Pilate; he suffered and was buried. And the third day he rose again, according to the scriptures; he ascended into heaven and sits at the right hand of the Father. And he shall come again with glory to judge the living and the dead; of his kingdom there shall be no end. And I believe in the Holy Spirit, Lord and giver of life, who proceeds from the Father and the Son. Who with the Father and Son together is worshiped and glorified; who has spoken through the Prophets. And I believe in one holy, catholic, and apostolic Church. I confess one baptism for the remission of sins. And I look for the resurrection of the dead, and the life of the world to come. Amen.

The church of Santa Maria della Salute (Saint Mary of Good Health) combines traditional Byzantine and western European design. The church was built by order of the Senate, to give thanks for the end of a terrible plague that killed one third of Venice's citizens in 1630. Every year on November 21, a temporary floating bridge was laid across the Grand Canal leading to the open doors of "La Salute" so that Venetians could walk across the water to offer prayers and thanks.

A Selection of Saints

Like many Christians today, Christians of the Middle Ages and Renaissance honored a large number of saints. The saints were people who had lived exceptionally holy lives and who had the power to perform miracles. Saints were believed to dwell in heaven, but they were not deities—God was the only divine power in the universe. However, God was often felt to be unreachable. So if a Christian needed something, she or he might pray to a saint instead of praying to God.

When seeking a saint's help, a person often prayed before a picture or statue of the saint or, if possible, at the saint's tomb or at a shrine dedicated to the saint. Some shrines housed relics—physical remains (usually bones)—of the saint. Holy relics had a great reputation for miraculous powers. During the Middle Ages Venetian churches acquired the remains of more than fifty saints.

People, countries, cities, churches, and craft guilds usually had one or more patron saints. The patron saint was the special protector of the person or group, who would in turn be especially devoted to that saint. Often a patron saint was chosen because of some similarity between an event in the saint's life and the activities of a particular group. For example, since Saint Joseph had been a carpenter, woodworkers of various kinds—including Venetian shipbuilders—regarded him as their patron saint.

The Miracle of the Relic of the True Cross *by Vittore Carpaccio illustrates a legend about a relic, a piece of the cross on which Jesus died. Thanks to the power of the relic, Venice's bishop was able to heal a man who had been suffering from mental illness (upper left).*

The Blessed Virgin

The most important saint was Mary, the mother of Jesus. Many churches in Venice were dedicated to her. Mary was known as the Blessed Virgin because she had never had relations with a man when she became pregnant with Jesus. Instead, her pregnancy began when the Holy Spirit entered her at the Annunciation. Mary was also called the Mother of God, the Queen of Heaven, and Our Lady. Italians often addressed her as Madonna, "My Lady."

The Gospels tell very little about Mary's life before and after the birth of Jesus. She was present at his first miracle, when he turned water into wine at a wedding banquet. She also visited him at least once while he was preaching, and she stood at the foot of the cross when he was crucified.

Many legends and traditions added to Mary's story. It was said that her mother had promised to dedicate her to God, so Mary was presented at the Temple in Jerusalem when she was three years old. When she was twelve, the high priest, instructed by an angel, called together all the widowers of the country. Each man was to bring a wooden rod and give it to the high priest. As Joseph handed over his rod, a dove flew from it and perched on his head. This was a sign that God had chosen him to be Mary's husband.

The legends also told that when Mary lay dying, the Holy Spirit brought all the disciples to her bedside. Jesus appeared, and she asked him to promise that everyone who prayed to her would receive mercy. Once her request was granted, she died. She was immediately taken up to heaven, body and soul, to reign beside her son.

The Winged Lion

The patron saint of Venice was Saint Mark, the author of the second Gospel. The Venetians were fiercely devoted to him. They frequently referred to their state as the Republic of Saint Mark. The saint's symbol, a winged lion, was also the symbol of Venice, appearing on all government buildings and on the republic's flags.

According to tradition, St. Mark traveled a great deal to spread the teachings of Jesus. When his mission took him into the Adriatic, a storm blew his ship onto one of the islands in the Venetian lagoon. An angel appeared to him and predicted that his body would one day rest on that site, where a great city would be built in his honor.

Saint Mark eventually became the first bishop of Alexandria, Egypt,

Saint Catherine of Alexandria presents the baby Jesus to Mary in this painting by Titian.

and there he died and was buried. But in 828 two Venetian merchants in Alexandria feared that local Muslims would destroy the saint's tomb. The merchants stole Saint Mark's mummified body, smuggling it out of Egypt. They took the holy remains home and presented them to the doge. After this Saint Mark was credited with performing many miracles in Venice.

On several other occasions Venetians went out of their way to bring holy relics back to their city. For example, after the First Crusade the Venetian fleet stopped in Asia Minor to acquire the body of Saint Nicholas, the patron saint of sailors. At the same time the Venetians obtained the remains of Saint Theodore.

Saint Theodore had been the city's patron before Saint Mark, and he continued to hold a place of honor. According to

SAINT MARK AND THE FISHERMAN

A Venetian legend tells how Saint Mark, in disguise, persuaded a poor fisherman to take him out into the lagoon in the middle of a storm. They stopped at the islands of San Niccolò di Lido and San Giorgio Maggiore to pick up Saint Nicholas and Saint George. Then they made for the open sea. There they met a galley full of demons, who were on their way to destroy Venice. The three saints battled and overcame the demons. After the fisherman took Saint Nicholas and Saint George back to their islands, Saint Mark gave him a ring and told him to present it to the doge as proof of the miraculous happenings.

legend, Theodore was a Roman soldier who was killed for his faith. He had lived an extremely righteous and heroic life and was said to have killed an evil dragon. Many Venetians were also very devoted to Saint George, another dragon-slaying saint.

Living the Faith

Ordinary Christians rarely aspired to the great holiness of the saints, but most did their best to follow the Church's teachings. They also attended church frequently to hear Mass. Much of this worship service, held every day, was sung by the priests and choir. The words were in Latin, the official language of the Catholic Church. On Sundays the priest might also preach a sermon, which explained biblical teachings and urged the congregation to live according to them.

The high point of the Mass was Holy Communion. This commemorated the Last Supper, the meal Jesus ate with his disciples before he was arrested and crucified. He had given them bread and wine, telling them that these were his body and blood, and bid them eat and drink in memory of him. At Communion the priest gave specially blessed bread to the congregation, saying, "This is the body of Christ." Wine was also blessed in the name of Christ, but only the priests drank it.

Both at church and at home, prayer was a major part of worship.

People often prayed straight from the heart, but they also used set Latin prayers. The most important of these was the Paternoster (Our Father), or Lord's Prayer. In the Gospel According to Matthew, Jesus teaches this prayer to his followers. The second most important prayer was the Ave Maria (Hail Mary). It was based largely on the angel Gabriel's words to the Virgin Mary at the Annunciation, recorded in the Gospel According to Luke.

Signs of Grace

Holy Communion was (and is) one of the seven sacraments of the Catholic Church. The sacraments were rituals or ceremonies that both demonstrated God's grace and bestowed it on those taking part in the sacrament.

Soon after birth, a baby was welcomed into the Church by the sacrament of Baptism. The child was sprinkled with holy water, anointed with holy oil, and blessed in the name of God the Father, the Son, and the Holy Spirit. The parents and godparents pledged to raise the child to live according to the Church's teachings. At the sacrament of Confirmation, around the age of thirteen, the child publicly renewed the vows made for him or her at baptism.

In the sacrament of Confession or Penance, a person confessed his or her sins to God through a priest. The priest would assign a penance for the person to perform in order to atone for the sins. Often the penance took the form of saying a certain number of prayers. A Catholic could not receive Holy Communion without first going to Confession.

The other sacrament that every Catholic expected to go through was Extreme Unction. A person who was thought to be close to death would make a last confession to a priest. After this confession the priest granted forgiveness of sins, while anointing the person's eyes, ears, nostrils, mouth, hands, and feet with holy oil.

Most people also took part in the sacrament of Matrimony, or marriage. But priests, monks, and nuns were not allowed to marry. With the sacrament of Holy Orders, they dedicated their lives to serving the Church.

This beautiful container was made somewhere in the Middle East but became one of the treasures of the Basilica of Saint Mark. It was said to contain some of the blood Jesus shed when he died.

CHAPTER FOUR

VENICE FIRST

The Venetians took tremendous pride in their republic—in its wealth and power, its government, and its long centuries of independence. For most of Venice's history, nothing was more important to its citizens than serving and glorifying their city, and sustaining the trade on which it thrived.

Church and State

Christianity was firmly woven into the fabric of Venetian society. As part of his office, the doge attended a multitude of religious functions every year, visiting many of the city's seventy parish churches. By 1581 Venice also had twenty-eight convents and thirty-one monasteries, where thousands of women and men lived out their lives in religious service. Large numbers of middle-class men were active members of religious organizations called *scuole* (skoo-OH-lay). Each *scuola* (skoo-OH-lah) was devoted to a particular saint, and religious services were held as part of meetings.

Venetian coins were imprinted with images of Jesus and Saint Mark, who was often shown presenting his banner to the current doge. Naval commanders had their ships' flags blessed on the altar of the Basilica of Saint Mark. Such practices differed little from Christian customs in the rest of western Europe. But the Venetian version of Catholicism had other features that were unique.

Independence from the Pope

It was said that the Venetians believed deeply in Saint Mark, a great deal in God, but hardly at all in the pope. During the Middle Ages and Renaissance, the pope ruled a large amount of Italian territory, and the Venetians were not about to let any foreign ruler exercise power over their republic.

Several times, in response to various acts of defiance, the pope

Leonardo Loredan, portrayed here by Giovanni Bellini, was doge from 1501 to 1521. When the other great powers of Europe banded together to attack Venice in the League of Cambrai, Loredan set an example of patriotism for the rest of the nobility. He ordered that his metal plates, platters, and silverware be melted down to fund the republic's war effort.

excommunicated the entire city of Venice. This meant that no one in the city was allowed to take part in any of the seven sacraments. To most Catholics excommunication was a dire punishment, for without the sacraments there was no access to God's grace. However, the priests and people of Venice routinely ignored the pope's decrees of excommunication and continued to worship as usual. The legends about Saint Mark and his special relationship with their city upheld the Venetians' sense of independence from the pope.

This independence was shown in many other ways, too. For example, all sentences pronounced by Church courts had to be ratified by one of the republic's courts. Whenever the Great Council discussed any kind of religious matter, all relatives and friends of the pope and other high Church officials were required to leave. It was the Venetian Senate, not the Church, that selected the bishop who oversaw Venice. Priests were never allowed to hold government office.

The Venetians never compromised when it came to the right to govern themselves. If there was a choice to be made between the demands of the republic and the demands of the Church, the republic won every time. As the people of Venice proudly declared, "We are Venetians first, then Christians."

Nobles, Citizens, and the People

Venetian society was divided into three classes, the *nobili* (NOH-bee-lee), or nobles; the *cittadini originari* (chee-tah-DEE-nee oh-ree-jee-NAH-ree), meaning "original citizens"; and the *popolani* (poh-poh-LAH-nee), the common people. In 1586 there were approximately 150,000 residents of Venice. Of these, only 4 percent belonged to the noble class and 5 percent to the *cittadini*. It was very difficult to move up in social class. In 1297 the Great Council was "closed" to new members, so it became impossible for men of common birth to join the noble class. Some women, though, could still marry into noble families. We have less information about the *cittadini originari*, but it seems that this class was also closed. During the sixteenth century, however, the government created two new categories of *cittadini* (one for Venetians and one for tax-paying foreigners), granting rights of citizenship to many merchants and educated professionals. This new "citizenship by privilege" also had its limits—it was open only to men who had never done any kind of manual labor.

Nobili

Nearly all Venetian nobles, or patricians, were merchants. Some also worked in banking, insurance, or law. Because of the risks of trade, Venetian nobles might be extremely wealthy or quite poor. Yet rich or poor, all patricians were considered equal to one another, all bearing the simple title *nobilomo*, "nobleman."

A portrait of a Venetian nobleman by Giovanni Bellini. For many centuries, the nobles of Venice dressed with a plain dignity that reflected their serious commitment to the good of the republic.

47

Service to the state was the patrician's duty and highest calling. From the age of twenty-five until his death, every nobleman was considered a member of the Great Council that governed Venice. During the course of his career the Great Council might elect him to a number of offices. Many offices, such as ambassador or provincial governor, required the nobleman to spend substantial sums of his own money. These positions could be held by only the wealthiest of the *nobili*.

Venetian nobles had few special privileges. During hard times, the state's first actions were to raise taxes on the patricians and cut payments to government officials. The laws of Venice applied equally to nobles and commoners. In fact, law-breaking patricians were often dealt with more harshly than commoners.

Marriage among the nobles was strictly regulated. If a woman from a noble family married a commoner, their sons were not permitted to serve in the Great Council. The only non-noble women who were approved to marry patrician men were women of the *cittadini* class and those whose fathers were master glassmakers.

Nobles were expected to live up to a very high standard of behavior, always upholding the honor of the republic. Their conservative code of conduct gave the Venetian state tremendous stability. And because the *nobili* placed so many restrictions on themselves, the other classes were all the more content to leave government solely in the nobles' hands.

Cittadini Originari

The *cittadini originari* were Venice's upper middle class. The men belonging to this class worked as merchants, bankers, doctors, pharmacists, lawyers, notaries, landlords, and businessmen. The *cittadini* also manned the Venetian civil service. They were secretaries to the Great Council, the Senate, the Council of Ten, and to the empire's naval commanders, ambassadors, and governors.

The *scuole grandi*, which were the six largest *scuole*, were the special domain of the *cittadini*. Here they had a kind of republic within the republic, electing their own officials and bestowing honors on deserving members. They hired the finest artists to decorate their meeting halls, which were among the most ornate buildings in Venice. The *scuole grandi* sponsored numerous building projects, made donations to churches, gave free apartments to impoverished members, provided dowries for

Pharmacists, members of the upper middle class, made and sold medicines and also sometimes treated patients. This pharmacist appears to be applying medicine for a toothache.

girls who otherwise could not afford to marry, and distributed money to the poor. In these ways the *scuole grandi* and their members earned the respect of all segments of Venetian society.

Popolani

The *popolani* were artisans, shopkeepers, sailors, fishers, laborers, chimney sweeps, musicians, actors, and merchants. Although the *popolani* had no say in the ruling of Venice, the government recognized the importance of their contributions to the republic.

Master artisans were particularly honored, with glassmakers and the Arsenal craftsmen the most privileged of all. The Arsenal workers were trained to bear arms and, when necessary, they served as a police force, a national guard, and as firefighters. They played important ceremonial roles, too. When a doge died, they were the torchbearers at his funeral. During a new doge's coronation, fifty Arsenal craftsmen carried him around Saint Mark's Square on a platform on their shoulders.

Every craft and trade, even the lowliest, had a guild. Guilds

This sign for the guild of Arsenal workers shows some of the great shipyard's master carpenters at work. Because ships were so important to Venice, the Arsenal workers were highly honored and respected.

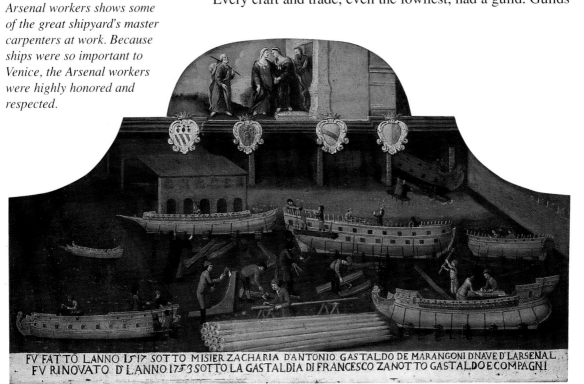

FV FATTO LANNO 1517 SOTTO MISIER ZACHARIA D'ANTONIO GASTALDO DE MARANGONI D'NAVE D'LARSENAL FV RINOVATO D'LANNO 1753 SOTTO LA GASTALDIA DI FRANCESCO ZANOTTO GASTALDOECOMPAGNI

were workers' associations that set standards for products, provided pensions for members' widows, and looked after members' interests in other ways. One of the guilds' most important functions was to regulate the training of apprentices, or student craftsmen. Beginning at age twelve, apprentices spent five to seven years learning their trade from a master. Two or three more years of supervised work followed before they could become master craftsmen themselves.

The common people had their own *scuole*, modeled upon those of the *cittadini*. Many poor *popolani* benefitted from the *scuole*'s charity. The Church and state also made provisions for the poor. For example, the *ospedali* where girls were trained as singers and musicians not only housed and educated orphans but also offered free treatment for the sick, pharmacies open to the public, and lodging for both men and women.

Venetian Women

Venice produced a number of talented women artists, musicians, and writers. But the majority of Venetian women received very little education. They were permitted no roles in government and few in society. Most were under the constant authority of a father, husband, or other male guardian. Women's lower status was supported by the traditions and laws of the Church, which preached that men were closer to God than women were.

Normally the only property a woman legally controlled was her dowry—the money and goods she brought into marriage. Usually, however, her husband managed her dowry. All household possessions—even her clothes—were owned by her husband. But despite women's lack of choice and control in marriage, a great many wives and husbands developed affectionate and respectful relationships.

Noblewomen and Nuns

During the Middle Ages and most of the Renaissance, women of the patrician class lived in very restricted conditions. Married women rarely left the house. Unmarried noblewomen never went out at all, except to attend Mass, and even then they were accompanied by a chaperon. Only in the seventeenth century did patrician women gain the freedom to enjoy Venice's operas, plays, concerts, and cafés.

Two women, dressed in the height of Venetian fashion, sun themselves on a balcony and play with their pets in this 1510 painting by Vittore Carpaccio.

Noble fathers tended to strongly prefer sons over daughters. A son could inherit and carry on the family business, while a daughter would marry into someone else's family. In order to marry, she had to be provided with a costly dowry. If a father had several daughters, he often provided dowries for only one or two. The rest were sent to convents to become nuns, who took vows of poverty, chastity, and obedience.

Many women thrived on the discipline of the convent, the opportunity to devote themselves to prayer and study, and the freedom from marriage and childbearing. But to many others, the convents were prisons. During the Renaissance, Venetian nuns were notorious for breaking convent rules—going out into the city, receiving male visitors, wearing fine clothes, lavishly decorating their rooms, and feasting on rich foods.

Women at Work

Women of the lower classes rarely became nuns. Poor women might labor for years, usually as servants, to earn dowry money. Many lower-class married women not only kept house and cared for their children but also earned wages. Usually they worked at home at jobs such as spinning, weaving, and lacemaking. Women who were the daughters, wives, or widows of craftsmen might work at the family trade in between their household duties. Some women labored outside the home, as servants, midwives, bead makers, water sellers, and so on.

A few Venetian women, usually from *cittadini originari* families, were able to make important contributions to the arts. Some of these women hosted sophisticated gatherings of artists, musicians, philosophers, and writers. Many were talented singers, musicians, composers, or writers themselves. For example, Polissena Pecorina was a famous singer and musician who performed at many notable gatherings during the 1500s. Veronica Franco and Gaspara Stampa were Renaissance Venice's greatest poets. In the seventeenth century, Barbara Strozzi had an extremely successful career as a singer and composer. Her works are being rediscovered and enjoyed by many music lovers today.

Multicultural Mix

As an international trading center, Venice was always full of people from other cities and countries. In fact, foreigners made up a full 10 percent of

IF YOU LIVED IN VENICE

If you had been born in the Venetian empire, your way of life would have been determined by the facts of your birth—whether you were a girl or a boy, a noble or a commoner, rich or poor, a slave or free. With this chart you can trace the course your life might have taken as a wealthy patrician in the fifteenth century.

You were born in Venice . . .

As a Boy . . .

As a Girl . . .

You live with your parents, brothers, and sisters in a spacious apartment. Your family has a number of servants. One of these is a woman who nurses you until you are two years old. As soon as you are old enough, your mother begins to teach you to read.

At age 7 you begin your formal education. You may go to school, or a tutor may come to the house. Your father, a merchant, begins to teach you about business and citizenship.

As a teenager you may spend some time at a monastery, studying with the monks. Possibly you will decide to become a monk or priest yourself. You may go to the University of Padua, where you can study mathematics, astronomy, philosophy, and law. In your late teens you go to sea for the first time, accompanying your father or one of his business partners on a trading voyage.

As a young man you spend many years in one of the overseas offices of your father's business. If you do not become a merchant, you may have a career in banking, law, or the military.

In your thirties or forties you settle down in Venice and marry. Your marriage is arranged by your father and the father of your bride. You may run your own business or take over the family business. You begin your career of service to the republic, attending meetings of the Great Council and filling minor government posts. You are elected to more and more important offices. At home, you teach your sons to follow in your footsteps.

At age 7 you spend most of your time with your mother, learning how to run a household. A tutor may come to the house to give you some education in literature and similar subjects. You may also learn to sing and play the lute. You leave the house only to go to church.

As a teenager you are old enough to get married, unless your father has already sent you to a convent to become a nun. Your father chooses your husband and gives you a dowry—money, household items, and other goods—to take with you to your new home. Your husband is probably about twice your age.

As a young married woman you give birth to many children. You give your children their first lessons in manners and morals. You supervise the servants and keep track of the household goods and food supply. You are a faithful and obedient companion to your husband.

In your thirties and forties you are probably widowed. If your sons are still young, you may help them learn their father's business. You may invest in merchant voyages and make small loans to relatives. Eventually you remarry. Once again your family chooses your husband. The children from your first marriage remain part of their father's family.

Most people do not live much beyond the age of fifty. When you die, your body is buried in a cemetery on one of the lagoon islands. Your family arranges for masses to be said at the parish church for the sake of your soul.

the city's residents. Visitors from elsewhere in Europe found Venice's multicultural atmosphere exotic. To the Venetians, however, multiculturalism was simply a fact of life—and of business.

In the fourteenth century the Venetian government established the Fondaco dei Tedeschi (the German Business Center) on the Rialto. In this state-owned building, German and Austrian merchants lived and sold their goods when they were in Venice. The Fondaco dei Tedeschi provided the model for *fondaci* (fohn-DAH-chee) for merchants from Florence, Milan, Persia, and Turkey. There were also English, Dalmatian, Albanian, and Armenian communities in different parts of the city. The city's largest foreign population was Greek. By the sixteenth century Venice's Greek community had its own church and was partially self-governing.

The Jewish Community

A large number of Jews lived in the Venetian empire, especially on the Greek island of Corfu and in Venice itself. Like other Christian Europeans, Venetians had many prejudices against Jews. However, business concerns were of prime importance in Venice, and the Jewish community came to play a major role in Venetian business. This fact, combined with the republic's traditional attitude of religious independence, led Venice to be far more tolerant toward the Jews than other European states were.

Church law prohibited Jews from owning land and restricted the way they could earn a living. At the same time Christians were generally forbidden to make loans and charge interest. Jews were therefore able to play an important role as bankers and moneylenders. Many also found ways to get around the laws and participate in trades from which they were officially barred.

In 1516 Venice's rulers decided that all Jews must live in the same part of the city, a walled-in area called the Ghetto. Jews were required to remain within the Ghetto walls after sundown, at least partly to protect them from possible anti-Jewish violence. But during the day Venice's Jews continued to be a powerful presence on the Rialto. By the end of the sixteenth century, along with their banking activities, they played an important role in the trade in spices, sugar, and cloth. Although Venetians were not totally free from prejudice, for centuries their empire remained the safest place in Europe for Jews.

VENICE AND SLAVERY

At the very bottom of the social scale were slaves. Venetian merchants bought and sold slaves beginning in the tenth century or earlier. Some slaves came from Africa, but many more were from eastern Europe. It was not unusual for the Venetians to have slaves. Most nations throughout history practiced slavery at one time or another.

Most of the slaves bought by Venetian traders were resold in the Byzantine Empire and Muslim countries. A great number, however, were taken to Venice or one of its territories. Some slaves worked in households or as boatmen, rowing the gondolas that carried well-to-do Venetians from place to place. Less fortunate slaves ended up working on the sugar plantations of Crete and Cyprus. Others labored on the great farms of Venice's territories on the Italian mainland.

This type of slavery disappeared from Venice and its empire during the 1500s. The same period, however, saw the appearance of slave rowers in the republic's galleys. Earlier in Venice's history the rowers had been free men, who often doubled as soldiers. When it became difficult to find free men willing to take the job, the rowing benches were filled with debtors and criminals. Then the republic's wars with the Ottoman Empire provided a large number of war prisoners, and soon these men were chained to the rowing benches. (The Turks also used prisoners of war, including Venetians, to row their ships.) Conditions were horrible. A galley slave's only hope of freedom was that the ship he was rowing would be captured by his own people.

Pageantry and Festivals

The Venetians' pride in their republic was encouraged and celebrated by the city's many festivals and ceremonies. The doge's official visits to different parts of the city were all opportunities for elaborate pageantry. The sailing and return of the *mudas* often became public holidays. Saint Mark's Square was the scene of frequent processions.

A number of major Christian holidays recalled events in the lives of Jesus and Mary—the Feast of the Annunciation, the Feast of the Resurrection (Easter), the Feast of the Nativity (Christmas), and others. In addition, each day of the year was dedicated to at least one saint. Every church, *scuola*, and guild celebrated the feast day of its patron saint. The

Feast of Saint Mark, on April 25, was a festival for the entire republic.

February 2 was the Feast of the Purification of the Virgin Mary. In 1300 this became the occasion for the first regatta, in which galleys raced on the Grand Canal. The regatta quickly became an annual event, showcasing Venetian seamanship. Eventually there were four regular regattas a year.

The longest celebration in Venice was Carnival, which lasted from December 26 to the beginning of Lent (the forty days before Easter). During Carnival people went about the city in masks, shedding their everyday identities. Rich and poor, nobles and commoners, women and men, citizens and foreigners alike attended theaters, concerts, balls, and casinos. The city's squares were full of music and dancing into the night, and work was suspended for days at a time.

The Marriage of the Sea

The Venetians were always conscious that they owed their wealth and power to their dominance of the sea. That dominance had been assured when Doge Pietro Orseolo II defeated the pirates of Dalmatia. His fleet had set sail on Ascension Day, the celebration of Jesus' ascending to heaven, in the year 1000. From then on, every year on Ascension Day Venice held a ceremony in which the city's bishop solemnly blessed the sea.

Early in the thirteenth century another element was added to the Ascension Day ceremony. This was the Marriage of the Sea, and it became a truly spectacular event. Accompanied by the bishop and other notable men, the doge boarded the *Bucintoro* (boo-chin-TOH-roh), the lavishly decorated state galley. He took his place on a throne under a rich red canopy, and one hundred Arsenal craftsmen slowly rowed the *Bucintoro* into the lagoon. The galley was escorted by crowds of boats of all types, many of them decked out with ribbons and other finery. Choirs sang, trumpets blasted, and all the church bells of Venice rang.

At the Porto de Lido, where the lagoon emptied into the open sea, the *Bucintoro* halted. The doge rose from his throne and faced the waters of the Adriatic. Solemnly he proclaimed, "We wed thee, O Sea, as a sign of our true and perpetual dominion." Then he removed a gold wedding ring from his finger and threw it into the water, once more sealing the bond between Venice and the sea.

The Bucintoro *makes ready to leave the Doge's Palace for the annual Marriage of the Sea. The water is crowded with boatloads of people, rich and poor, ready to spend the day celebrating. The artist, Canaletto, specialized in painting scenes of Venice's landmarks and festivities.*

CHAPTER FIVE

A LASTING BRILLIANCE

After Napoleon conquered Venice in 1797, he handed the city over to Austrian rule. Seventy years later Austria was defeated in the Austro-Prussian War, and the Venetians were given the opportunity to decide their future. They voted to join the new Kingdom of Italy, which had formed in 1861. Venice has been part of Italy ever since.

Still, visitors to the city are impressed by how different Venice is from the rest of Italy—and not simply because it has canals instead of roads. The pace is slower, and so is the rate of change. Although Napoleon's soldiers stripped the city of many of its ornaments, it still looks much as it did during the Renaissance. The Venetians speak a distinct form of Italian, as they always have. They continue their ancestors' traditions of fine craftsmanship, love of festivals, and pride in their city. In Venice a sense of history is everywhere.

A Model State

During the centuries when Venice was a great power, it played a major part in European politics and economics. Its role in the Crusades and in other wars helped shape history. So did its status as a mediator between East and West and between the Holy Roman Empire and the Church.

Venice left a lasting mark on the lands that made up its empire. Venetian buildings still stand on many of the Greek islands and in the cities of the eastern Adriatic coast. Some of these cities, such as Split in Croatia, developed substantially under Venetian rule and remain thriving seaports. Numerous words in modern spoken Greek come from the Venetian dialect of Italian, and nearly all the words that deal with ships and sailing are pure Venetian.

The trade that nourished the Republic of Saint Mark also benefitted its trading partners. From the Middle Ages to the Renaissance there was a general increase in prosperity throughout Europe. Long-distance trade

Venice's unique beauty has been an inspiration to artists from many countries. This canal scene is by nineteenth-century Belgian painter Franz Richard Unterberger.

BROUGHT TO YOU BY THE VENETIANS

Venice was responsible for bringing many Eastern products to western Europe. From there they were later taken to the Americas and Australia. Chances are that every day you wear, eat, or use something that the Venetians made part of European culture.

Venetian merchants were the West's foremost importers of silk and cotton. For at least two centuries, Venice was virtually the only European importer of spices, especially pepper. Sugar and raisins were among the other Eastern foods that Venetian merchants brought to Europe.

Venice also introduced the West to a new way to eat. When a Byzantine princess married the doge's son in 1005, she brought a two-pronged eating utensil with her to Venice. Before long all wealthy Venetians were using forks. The innovation took five hundred years to catch on in the rest of Europe.

In the 1560s coffee was introduced to Venice from Turkey. Soon the city was full of coffee houses, with twenty-four in Saint Mark's Square alone. These cafés were popular meeting places, where people chatted, flirted, and debated for hours. The Venetian fashion for cafés and coffee drinking spread all over Europe and continues today. It's become popular in America, too.

distributed food supplies and goods to many lands, giving people access to things they could not produce in their own regions. The opportunity to export foods and manufactured items gave communities new sources of income. In these ways Venetian merchants helped create a world in which the economies of all countries were connected, laying the foundations of today's global economy.

Alongside the flow of trade, Venice also circulated ideas. The republic's political ideals influenced the way many people thought about government. The Venetians' devotion to the good of the state offered Europeans an inspiring model of patriotism. Venice's constitution was studied and admired, for the republic was virtually the only state in medieval and Renaissance Europe that was not governed by a hereditary ruler. Moreover, the republic had a careful system of checks and balances so that no part of the government could become too powerful. The writers of the United States Constitution may well have taken inspiration from these features of Venetian government.

Cultural Contributions

Achievements and advancements in the arts are among Venice's greatest legacies. In 1565 Venice opened the world's first commercial theater, built specifically for plays put on for a paying audience. The world's first public opera house followed in 1637. Concerts performed by professional musicians—again, for a ticket-buying public—were another Venetian innovation.

The art, music, and theater of Venice were extremely influential throughout Europe. Works by the great Venetian painters were in demand in Spain, France, and Germany as well as

Nobles enjoy a special dinner at the Theater of San Beneto in the 1700s. It was the fourth theater built in Venice and was very famous.

throughout Italy. By the sixteenth century outstanding artists such as Crete's El Greco (who later settled in Spain) and Germany's Albrecht Dürer were coming to Venice to learn the Venetian style of painting. Musicians and composers also came to Venice to study. For example, George Frederick Handel, most famous today for the "Hallelujah Chorus," spent time in Venice in the eighteenth century.

Both commedia dell'arte and the new form of comic theater developed by Carlo Goldoni were immensely popular in Paris and other cities. Commedia dell'arte spread as far as Turkey, Poland, and Russia. Venetian opera also left its mark, setting the standard for opera throughout the seventeenth and into the eighteenth centuries.

Books for Everyone

During the decades surrounding 1500, Venice served as the publishing capital of Europe. The printing press had been invented in Germany, by Johannes Gutenberg, in the 1450s. A decade later Venetian craftsmen were setting up their own presses. Soon there were Venetian publishers specializing in ancient Greek and Roman literature, in science and mathematics, and in music books. With its flourishing Greek community, Venice became Europe's largest publisher of Greek books. Great numbers of Hebrew books were produced in the Ghetto. The publication of maps, illustrated medical books, and popular fiction was pioneered in Venice.

Venetian books were exported to London, Constantinople, and numerous cities in between. Whereas books had previously been completely handmade and available only to the very wealthy, now almost anyone could afford to buy a book. Information and ideas of all kinds circulated through Europe as never before—largely thanks to the publishers of Venice.

Advancing Knowledge

Venice also contributed to the world of knowledge through the University of Padua, in northeastern Italy. During the fifteenth through eighteenth centuries the university was directly controlled by the Venetian government. The Church was allowed very little influence. This set Padua apart from all other European universities. Open discussion and differing viewpoints were actively encouraged, and people of many faiths were welcomed as students.

The University of Padua's forward-looking attitude toward research and education led to a number of major advances. Andreas Vesalius, a professor at Padua, began the practice of teaching human anatomy by dissecting corpses. Vesalius and his followers gave European doctors their first accurate understanding of the human body. Padua's professors were also the first to teach medicine by having students work directly with sick people. For these reasons Padua is often called the birthplace of modern medicine.

Galileo Galilei made the University of Padua the birthplace of modern astronomy as well. While he was a professor there, he invented the telescope and with it discovered Jupiter's four largest moons. Galileo's work proved the theories of Nicolaus Copernicus, an earlier student at Padua. Copernicus had proposed

Galileo Galilei demonstrates his telescope to the doge and the dogal councillors. In 1609 Galileo's telescope showed him that the Moon had mountains and pits instead of a completely smooth surface, as people had previously believed. In 1610, thanks again to his telescope, Galileo became the first person to see the four largest moons of Jupiter.

the theory that the Earth was not the center of the universe, but that instead it and the other planets orbit around the Sun.

The University of Padua, which still exists, was acknowledged as Europe's greatest center of learning from 1530 to 1630, and the medical school maintained its superior reputation long afterward. It continued to train Eastern Orthodox and Jewish doctors when other European institutions would not. In 1678 the University of Padua took another great stride: it became the first university to award the Doctor of Philosophy degree to a woman, the Venetian patrician Elena Cornaro Piscopia.

Leading the Way

Police and firefighting services, zoning, public health measures, public housing—these and many other institutions that we take for granted today were pioneered in Venice. The republic was also a trailblazer in finance, diplomacy, and industry.

Venice was the first European state to make large investments of public funds. The Arsenal, the merchant galley fleet, and a number of the city's essential industries were all supported by tax monies and loans made to the city. Throughout its history Venice depended on loans, made to the state on a regular basis by the *nobili*. Today deficit spending—the spending of public funds raised by loans—is practiced by governments around the world.

Many other financial arrangements that are common today were first explored by Venice and other Italian city-states. The bankers on the Rialto specialized in helping merchants transfer large sums of money through letters of credit, the forerunners of checks. Northern Italy's financial experts developed new, highly accurate methods of bookkeeping. They were also among the first in Europe to use Arabic numbers (1, 2, 3) instead of Roman numerals (I, II, III).

Venice's reliance on trade led to advances in the field of diplomacy. To maintain good international relations and stay informed on international conditions, the republic sent ambassadors to the foreign cities where it did business. Countries had sent ambassadors to other nations before, but always on specific missions. By 1450 Venice had permanent embassies in many cities. Ambassadors sent home regular reports and represented Venetian interests as necessary. Other states soon realized the

The Return of the English Envoys *by Vittore Carpaccio shows the great ceremony with which Venice welcomed foreign ambassadors.*

usefulness of having permanent embassies abroad. Today this is common practice.

Venice's industrial advances included one of Europe's earliest and most efficient production lines—the Arsenal. Ships were built and outfitted at the Arsenal using methods of mass production that were hundreds of years ahead of the times. Venice was also the first state to issue patents, guaranteeing inventors the sole rights to develop and market their inventions.

The Republic of Venice led the way in regulating child labor and protecting the poor from unfair treatment by the wealthy and powerful. In its mainland territories, it upheld the rights of free peasants against the great landowners. Venice pioneered the conservation of natural resources, too. For example, in the fifteenth century the government placed strict limits on timber harvesting and ordered the planting of oak seedlings on the mainland to replace cut timber.

City of Dreams

For centuries people have been drawn to Venice. During the republic's golden age, most visitors came for business purposes. Many others, however, visited Venice for religious reasons. In the Middle Ages and Renaissance, Christians often went on pilgrimages, journeys to important religious sites. Not only were pilgrimages believed to be good for a person's soul, but they also provided an opportunity to see new places and enjoy new experiences.

Venice's many churches, shrines, and saintly relics made the city a popular pilgrim destination. More importantly, Venice was an ideal starting point for the greatest of all pilgrimages, to Palestine, the Holy Land. Many Christians dreamed of visiting the places where Jesus lived, taught, and died. To help them fulfill this dream, two Venetian galleys every year voyaged to the Holy Land. For a fixed fee, pilgrims received round-trip passage to Palestine, transportation by donkey to and from Jerusalem, a guide and guards, and food for the entire trip. In all likelihood, this pilgrimage was the first package tour offered anywhere in Europe.

Venice's popularity with visitors helped make the republic a trailblazer of the tourist industry. The first guidebooks for tourists, published in Venice in the 1500s, were guides to the city's sights. Venice was becoming renowned for its elegant buildings, exotic atmosphere, beautiful art and music, and colorful ceremonies. More and more visitors came specifically to experience this unique city for themselves. Restaurants and inns flourished. The business of producing souvenirs also grew—in the eighteenth century many artists earned their living by painting Venetian scenes for tourists.

By the 1700s Venice had a reputation as a city of pleasure. Wealthy and adventurous people flocked there, especially during Carnival time, when they could be unknown behind their masks. They left their troubles behind at plays and operas. They gossiped in the cafés. They won and lost fortunes in elegant casinos, where they enjoyed music and dancing as well as gambling. In this city of dreams, they indulged themselves as they could never dream of doing at home.

VENICE IN THE ARTS

Once she did hold the gorgeous east in fee;
And was the safeguard of the west: the worth
Of Venice did not fall below her birth,
Venice, the eldest Child of Liberty.

—from "On the Extinction of the Venetian Republic," by William Wordsworth (1802)

Artists and writers have been visiting Venice since the Renaissance. They have studied and found inspiration there. Often they have made the city itself a part of their paintings, poems, and plays. Many who have never even laid eyes on the Grand Canal or Saint Mark's Square have experienced the inspiration of Venice.

No one knows whether William Shakespeare (1564–1616) ever spent time in Venice. But the city is the setting for two of his plays, *Othello* and *The Merchant of Venice*. Some of his other plays are set in Padua and Verona, both part of the Venetian Empire during Shakespeare's time.

William Wordsworth also may never have been to Venice. But "On the Extinction of the Venetian Republic" is judged one of his best poems, and it is certainly the greatest English poem about Venice. Other nineteenth-century English poets, including Lord Byron and Robert Browning, visited and wrote about the beautiful lagoon city.

One of the most notable non-Italian artists to portray the Venetian landscape was England's J. M. W. Turner (1775–1851). Turner visited Venice toward the end of his life and found it the ideal setting to explore the effects of light and color. Another famous nineteenth-century artist who spent time painting in Venice was the American James Whistler.

Many twentieth-century novels have used Venice as setting and inspiration. The most well known of these is probably *Death in Venice*, published in 1912 by the great German writer Thomas Mann. The Jewel of the Adriatic has also attracted filmmakers, who have featured the city in a number of movies. Among them are *From Russia with Love*, *Indiana Jones and the Last Crusade*, and *In Love and War*.

Masked revelers enjoy flirting and gambling at the Ridotto, one of Venice's state-owned casinos. This scene was painted by Francesco Guardi in the eighteenth century.

Preserving the Jewel

After Napoleon's conquest of Venice, the crowds of pleasure seekers fell away. Then, in the 1930s, Italian dictator Benito Mussolini built a causeway from the mainland to Venice, and travelers rediscovered the Jewel of the Adriatic. Today Venice hosts 11 million visitors a year. They are drawn by the city's history, its uniqueness, its beauty, its art and architecture. Many say

A modern Venetian Carnival mask shows the city's continued love of beauty, creativity, and festivity.

that Venice is simply one of the most romantic cities in the world.

However, Venice has been troubled for some time. Pollution from mainland industry is dulling and eroding many of the city's beautiful buildings. Waves from motorboats are damaging building foundations. The natural balance of the lagoon has been disturbed by deep channels cut for modern ships. And the city itself is very slowly sinking into the lagoon.

Fortunately Venice is a city that many people all over the world deeply love. A number of local and international efforts are now under way to restore and preserve the city. Hopes for its survival and continued brilliance are high. This ability to inspire dreams and great undertakings may well prove to be the heart and soul of the Venetian empire's legacy.

The Venetian Empire: A Time Line

In full sail, Venetian war galleys engage a Turkish fleet in 1689.

First Crusade **1095–1099**

Venice helps Byzantine Empire fight the Normans and is rewarded with special trading privileges **1081**

Defeat of Dalmatian pirates **1000**

Remains of Saint Mark brought to Venice **828**

Election of the first doge **697**

5th century C.E. First settlements on the islands of the Venetian lagoon

1200	1400	1600	1800

Venice surrenders to Napoleon; the city and all its possessions are given to Austria ●**1797**

The Turks retake southern Greece ● **1718**

Francesco Morosini reconquers southern Greece for Venice ●**1684**

Venice loses Cyprus to the Turks; defeat of Turkish navy at Battle of Lepanto ●**1571**

Turks gain naval supremacy with the defeat of Venice and ●**1538** its allies at the Battle of Preveza

Jews confined to the Ghetto ●**1516**

The League of Cambrai makes war against Venice ●**1508–1509**

Venice defeated by the Turks at Battle of Zonchio ● **1499**

● **1473** Venice gains control of Cyprus

Venice fights four wars for control of northeastern Italy ● **1425–1454**

● **1405** Venice conquers Verona and Padua

● **1378–1381** Fourth war with Genoa

● **1368** Venice gains Corfu

● **1355** Doge Marino Falier, would-be dictator, is beheaded

● **1347** Plague kills three-fifths of Venice's people

● **1330** Organization of the *mudas*

● **1310** Plot to overthrow the Venetian government; establishment of the Council of Ten

● **1257–1270** First war with Genoa

● **1240** Venice gains control of the eastern reach of the Po River

● **1202–1204** Fourth Crusade

● **1177** Venice hosts peace conference between the pope and Holy Roman Emperor Frederick Barbarossa

● **1171** All Venetians in the Byzantine Empire are arrested and their belongings are confiscated

● **1153** Venice's control over Istria is confirmed

● **1104** Founding of the Arsenal

GLOSSARY

Annunciation: the angel Gabriel's visit to the Virgin Mary to tell her that she had been chosen to bear the son of God

apostolic: having spiritual authority descended from Jesus' twelve apostles

artisan: an expert in a craft, such as a carpenter, glassblower, bead maker, or weaver

Ascension Day: a Catholic holiday celebrated the fortieth day after Easter, it commemorates Christ's ascending to heaven

Byzantine Empire: the successor of the eastern half of the ancient Roman Empire; its core was Asia Minor and Greece

cittadini originari (chee-tah-DEE-nee oh-ree-jee-NAH-ree): "original citizens"; the upper middle class

commedia dell'arte (koh-MAY-dee-uh dell AR-tay): a form of Italian theater in which masked actors playing stereotyped characters made up their own lines and actions

doge (doj): Italian for *duke*; in early times the ruler of Venice, in later times the republic's chief magistrate

dowry: money, goods, or property that a woman brings to her marriage

fondaco (fohn-DAH-koh), plural *fondaci* (fohn-DAH-chee): a state-owned building where foreign merchants lived, did business, and stored their goods

fresco: a wall painting made while the plaster is still wet

galley: a long, low, highly maneuverable ship that could be rowed or sailed

Ghetto: the walled-in area where Venice's Jews lived after 1516. (The name comes from the word *geto*, "foundry," because an iron-working factory had been located on the site.)

guild: an organization for people who practice the same craft or trade

Holy Roman Empire: an empire made up primarily of German, Austrian, and Italian territories, founded in 962 C.E. with the idea of unifying Europe. The emperor was usually also the German king.

lute: a musical instrument popular in the sixteenth and seventeenth centuries, with a pear-shaped body, short neck, and eleven strings. It is held like a guitar and played by plucking the strings.

mediator: a go-between, or someone who helps two disagreeing parties work out their differences

mezzanine (meh-zuh-NEEN): a shorter story located between two main stories of a building

Middle Ages: the period of European history from the sixth century to the fourteenth or fifteenth century

mosaic: a picture or design made by fitting together bits of stone, glass or tiny colored tiles, and cementing them in place

muda (MOO-dah): a state-organized trading voyage in which several great galleys traveled in a convoy on a specific route

nobili (NOH-bee-lee): the nobles

opera: a kind of elaborate play in which all the words are sung instead of spoken

ospedale (oh-speh-DAH-lay), plural *ospedali* (oh-speh-DAH-lee): "hospital"; a center that performed social services such as housing the poor, treating the sick, and educating orphans, including girls who were taught to sing, compose, and play instruments

parish: an area that has its own church and priest

pope: the bishop of Rome, head of the Catholic Church. During the Middle Ages and Renaissance the pope was also the ruler of a large portion of Italy.

popolani (poh-poh-LAH-nee): the common people

Renaissance: the period of European history from the fourteenth through seventeenth centuries

saint: a person recognized by the Church as being especially holy and able to perform miracles both in life and after death

scuola (skoo-OH-lah), plural *scuole* (skoo-OH-lay): a men's religious and charitable organization whose officers and members belonged to the *cittadini* and *popolani*; also, the building in which this organization met. Craft guilds and organizations for foreign residents of Venice might also be referred to as *scuole*.

FOR FURTHER READING

*Boulton, Susie. *Venice and the Veneto*. London and New York: Dorling Kindersley, 1995.

Chubb, Thomas Caldecott. *The Venetians: Merchant Princes*. New York: Viking, 1968.

Greene, Carol. *Marco Polo: Voyager to the Orient*. Chicago: Children's Press, 1987.

Kernaghan, Pamela, and Tony McAleavy. *The Crusades: Cultures in Conflict*. Cambridge and New York: Cambridge University Press, 1993.

Moore, Robert. *Living in Venice*. Morristown, New Jersey: Silver Burdett, 1986.

*Thubron, Colin, and the Editors of Time-Life Books. *The Venetians*. Alexandria, Virginia: Time-Life Books, 1980.

Ventura, Piero. *Venice: Birth of a City*. New York: Putnam, 1988.

Vernon, Roland. *Introducing Vivaldi*. Morristown, New Jersey: Silver Burdett, 1996.

*Although written for adults, this book contains much to interest younger readers as well.

ON-LINE INFORMATION*

Gable, C. I. *Art and Architecture of Venice*. [http://www.boglewood.com/cornaro/xcornaro.html].

Gable, C. I. *Virtual History of Venice*. [http://www.boglewood.com/timeline/].

Imboden, Durant. *Venice for Visitors*. [http://goeurope.tqn.com/travel/goeurope/mmore.htm].

Martin, Michael, ed. *Thesaurus Precum Latinarum: Treasury of Latin Prayers*. [http://unidial.com/~martinus/Thesaurus.html].

Raffael, Claudio. *The Web Site of Venice*. [http://www.venetia.it].

Van Zyverden, Juli. *Venice Italy Index*. [http://www.iuav.univ.it/~juli/venindx.html].

Venetian Ospedali. [http://music.acu.edu/www/iawm/pages/ospedali.html].

Venezia Net S. R. L. *Culture*. [http://www.doge.it/cultura/cultmeni.htm].

*Websites change from time to time. For additional on-line information, check with the media specialist at your local library.

BIBLIOGRAPHY

Ammerman, Albert J. "Probing the Depths of Venice" in *Archaeology* vol. 49 no. 4 (1996): pp. 39–43.

Brown, Howard M. *Music in the Renaissance.* Englewood Cliffs, New Jersey: Prentice-Hall, 1976.

Feist, Aubrey. *The Lion of St. Mark.* Indianapolis: Bobbs-Merrill, 1971.

Gies, Frances, and Joseph Gies. *Cathedral, Forge, and Waterwheel: Technology and Invention in the Middle Ages.* New York: HarperCollins, 1994.

Huse, Norbert, and Wolfgang Wolters. *The Art of Renaissance Venice: Architecture, Sculpture, and Painting, 1460–1590.* Trans. Edmund Jephcott. Chicago and London: University of Chicago Press, 1990.

Jardine, Lisa. *Worldly Goods: A New History of the Renaissance.* New York and Toronto: Doubleday, 1996.

King, Margaret L. *Women of the Renaissance.* Chicago and London: University of Chicago Press, 1991.

McEvedy, Colin. *The Penguin Atlas of Medieval History.* Harmondsworth: Penguin, 1961.

McNeill, William H. *Venice: The Hinge of Europe 1081–1797.* Chicago and London: University of Chicago Press, 1974.

Metford, J. C. J. *Dictionary of Christian Lore and Legend.* London: Thames and Hudson, 1983.

Morris, Jan. *The Venetian Empire: A Sea Voyage.* New York and London: Harcourt Brace Jovanovich, 1980.

Neuls-Bates, Carol, ed. *Women in Music: An Anthology of Source Readings from the Middle Ages to the Present.* New York: Harper & Row, 1982.

Palisca, Claude V. *Baroque Music,* 2d ed. Englewood Cliffs, New Jersey: Prentice-Hall, 1981.

Rosenthal, Margaret F. *The Honest Courtesan: Veronica Franco, Citizen and Writer in Sixteenth-Century Venice.* Chicago and London: University of Chicago Press, 1992.

Thubron, Colin, and the Editors of Time-Life Books. *The Venetians.* Alexandria, Virginia: Time-Life Books, 1980.

Zorzi, Alvise. *Venice: The Golden Age, 697–1797.* New York: Abbeville Press, 1983.

INDEX

Page numbers for illustrations are in boldface

ABOUT THE AUTHOR

Kathryn Hinds has been fascinated by cultures of the past for most of her life. As a child she dreamed of becoming an archaeologist—or a writer or an opera singer. She grew up near Rochester, New York, then moved to New York City to study music and writing at Barnard College. She did graduate work in comparative literature and medieval studies at the City University of New York. For several years she has worked as an author and freelance editor of children's books. Ms. Hinds now lives in the north Georgia mountains with her husband, their son, three cats, and three dogs. Her other books in this series are *Medieval England*, *The Vikings*, *The Incas*, *The Ancient Romans*, *The Celts of Northern Europe*, and *India's Gupta Dynasty*.

4/11 ⑥
7/15 ⑨ 5/16

HOW ANIMALS BEHAVE

A New Look at Wildlife

Disguised as a pink flower, a praying mantis—an insect— waits for a meal. When another insect comes near, the mantis will grab it. This mantis is shown six times actual size.

ANTHONY BANNISTER

BOOKS FOR WORLD EXPLORERS
NATIONAL GEOGRAPHIC SOCIETY

Contents

Copyright © 1984 National Geographic Society
Library of Congress CIP data: p. 104

BELOW: *On a tiny Hawaiian island, a Laysan albatross pair begin the series of steps that lead to mating. The bird on the left rapidly claps its bill open and shut as its mate sings to the sky.*

FRANS LANTING

PAGES 4–5: *Two African mountain gorillas peer through tangles of greenery. Read more about gorillas and how they live on pages 80 through 83.*

BOB CAMPBELL

Foreword

When I sit down to enjoy a book like this, I am impressed by the wealth of sound scientific information available to young readers today. In my school days, a book of similar quality and scope simply did not exist. Why? At that time, only a handful of scientists were working in the field of animal behavior. Most of them saw the actions of animals in terms of human needs and emotions. But a few were beginning to realize that it is the instinct to survive that underlies all animal behavior.

Extensive field study was required to confirm this new direction. It has been the National Geographic Society's great fortune to help sponsor scientific studies of animal behavior throughout the world. The African mountain gorillas on these pages are among the groups studied by Dian Fossey, whose pioneering work was funded in part by the Geographic. Other recipients of Society grants represented in this book include Jane Goodall, as well as William Franklin, Francine Patterson, and Merlin Tuttle.

I hope this book motivates young people to consider animal-behavior studies as a profession.

GILBERT M. GROSVENOR
President, National Geographic Society

T=1= he Need to Feed

By Jacqueline Geschickter

Food is at the top of an animal's survival list. The koala (left) spends most of its few waking hours eating. High in the treetops of eastern Australia, it feeds on only one thing — eucalyptus leaves. And because it gets most of the water it needs from the leaves, it seldom climbs down to the ground.

For a fresh supply of leaves, the koala leaps or climbs from treetop to treetop. The animal eats so many leaves every day that it takes a hundred big trees to keep a koala in food during its lifetime.

Everywhere in the world, animals use their special abilities and methods to get food. Some animals — wolves, Cape hunting dogs, and hyenas, for example — work together to chase and catch prey. Others, like tigers, are solitary hunters. Many kinds of spiders make traps to capture their dinners. A fish called an angler baits its prey. Whether animals harvest or hunt, trap or lure, they have developed an amazing variety of ways to obtain the food they need to survive.

Sea creatures called goose barnacles poke their arms out of their shells. The barnacles spread their arms and draw them together. Hairs on the arms strain tiny plants and animals from the water. Then the barnacles pull in their arms. The food tumbles off into their mouths.

Snug inside a mossy shelter, a flying squirrel gnaws an acorn. In summer, the animal eats mainly insects, berries, and mushrooms. As cold weather approaches, it begins collecting acorns and other nuts. By eating mostly stored food, the squirrel survives the winter.

Every animal on earth must eat to survive. Food provides an animal with energy. To stay alive, the animal must obtain more energy from its food than it uses in getting the food.

Some animals have methods of obtaining food that require little effort and save a lot of energy. Barnacles, for example, don't go after their food. These sea creatures fasten themselves to other sea animals or to underwater objects, such as pieces of wood or ships' bottoms. Ocean currents bring the barnacles their food.

With its feathery arms, a barnacle strains plankton—tiny sea animals and plants—out of the water. As the barnacle draws its arms back inside its body, the food tumbles off, into its mouth.

Getting food is not so simple for every animal as it is for the barnacle. During cold or dry seasons, most kinds of plants do not grow. At such times, the animals that feed on plants may not have enough to eat.

A Green Diet: The Plant-eaters

When food is scarce, some plant-eaters rely on food they have stored. During the winter, wild hamsters in Europe and Asia nibble seeds and vegetables tucked away inside their burrows.

Stores of acorns and other nuts help the tree squirrels and flying squirrels in North America survive the winter. North American beavers build underwater stockpiles of branches and slender trees.

These woodpiles supply them with bark to eat when snow and ice keep them in their lodges.

Other animals migrate, or travel, to areas where they can find food. All winter, reindeer live in mountains near the Arctic Ocean. There they feed on small plants called lichens (LIKE-uns) that live under the snow. In summer, the lichens dry up and die. So, as the weather warms up, the reindeer migrate northward. They move to colder areas, where lichens stay alive under a little snow.

Wildebeests, large African antelopes, feed on grasses. The animals graze about ten hours a day. As they rest, they bring up partly digested food—called a cud—and chew it again.

During the rainy season, the wildebeests share the southern

BOB CAMPBELL

Wildebeests graze on the Serengeti Plain in Africa. During the rainy season in the south of the plain, these large antelopes feed on green grasses. When the dry season comes, they migrate, or travel, to better pastures. A million wildebeests head northward. They return when rains again water the south.

part of the Serengeti Plain with many other animals, including zebras and small antelopes called Thomson's gazelles. When grass dries up on that part of the Serengeti, many of these animals migrate. They trek northward to greener pastures on slightly wooded plains. The animals don't return to the south until rain clouds signal the end of the dry season.

When the wildebeests arrive in the north, the zebra herds are already there. The zebras eat huge amounts of grass stalks that grow as tall as a person. After the zebras have chewed off a few feet of these bulky stalks, the lower leaves grow bigger. The arriving wildebeests pull off these leaves.

Wildebeests cannot eat as much as zebras do. The leaves they eat are less bulky than the stalks, but have more nourishment.

As the wildebeests tear off the leaves, they expose tiny, protein-rich plants growing close to the ground. These plants are food for the Thomson's gazelles. In this way, the zebras, the wildebeests,

9

Nectar provides fast fuel for a black-chinned hummingbird (right). The tiny bird, shown three times actual size, feeds at a trumpet creeper blossom. Hummingbirds also eat spiders from the blossoms. A hummingbird may visit 2,000 flowers a day.

Through its uncoiled, tubelike tongue, a Polyura butterfly sucks juice from rotting fruit (above). This insect lives on the island of New Guinea. With eyes that see colors and antennae that detect odors, it locates food.

and the Thomson's gazelles make use of the limited food supply.

A Taste for Sweets: The Nectar Feeders

Landing gently on a piece of fruit, a butterfly uncoils its long tongue to drink. A hummingbird hangs in the air, dipping its bill into a blossom. Both these animals drink sweet liquids that are quickly turned into energy.

Nectar, a sugary liquid produced by flowers, and other plant juices provide food for some small creatures. Butterflies, for example, suck nectar from blossoms and juices from rotting fruit. These liquids are their most important food, but they feed on other things, too. They drink muddy water for salts, and liquids from animal wastes for proteins. Some butterflies change flower pollen into a liquid, then drink it.

Both hummingbirds and small

10

tropical birds called honey eaters drink nectar. Hummingbirds hover in front of flower blossoms while they drink. Honey eaters sip through holes they peck at the bases of flowers.

Honeybees and bumblebees suck nectar through their tubelike tongues. Chemicals inside their bodies turn the nectar into honey.

Nearly all kinds of mosquitoes need sweet plant juices to stay alive. Often they drink nectar through holes already drilled in the blossoms by bees. To produce eggs, however, female mosquitoes must bite people or animals. They need the extra protein that comes from blood. Male mosquitoes, on the other hand, eat only fruit juices and nectar.

Even some bats feed on nectar. Inside the bats' pointed muzzles are long tongues for lapping up liquids. The animals fly down to the flowers, take speedy licks, and dart off to approach again.

11

A barn owl carries its catch—a mouse (left). This night hunter uses silence and surprise to obtain its food. Flying quietly over a field, it looks and listens for small creatures. When the owl finds a meal, it swoops down feetfirst. Legs extended and sharp claws held apart, it grabs its prey. The owl kills the animal with its beak, then flies off with the prize.

Night hides a prowling tiger in India (left). Walking on padded toes, the cat moves noiselessly. It creeps up on a deer, a wild pig, or other prey and then springs.

Dust flies as a zebra runs from a cheetah in Africa (right). The swift cheetah can keep up its lightning dash for only a short distance. Often that is long enough for it to overtake its prey and knock the animal down.

Nectar-feeding bats, however, are not as common as other kinds. You may have seen a bat during a warm summer night. It was probably searching for insects or other small creatures to eat. Most bats are predators—animals that catch and eat other animals for food.

In Pursuit of a Meal: The Predators

When a predator spots a meal, it cannot simply feast on it as a koala or a hummingbird can. Plants don't move, but the predator's meal—a living animal—usually tries to escape.

It takes hard work and skill for a predator to catch its prey. For example, the kingfisher, a bird, often makes several dives before it catches a fish. Scientists estimate that about 90 percent of a tiger's prey escapes. They have also found that wolves give up a chase nine times out of ten.

A barn owl's hunting success depends on the weather. This bird uses its eyes and ears as it hunts mice or other small animals. On clear, dry nights, when an owl can hear its prey scurrying through the grass or leaves, the bird may catch several mice. On rainy nights, however, the damp leaves and wet grass rustle less. Then the owl generally misses its targets and may go hungry.

Tigers, wolves, and some other large predators often do not eat for several days. When they do make

13

Gray wolves feast on a deer in Minnesota (left). Wolves work together to hunt large prey, such as deer, moose, elk, and caribou. If one caribou lags behind the herd, a wolf pack might chase it for miles across open ground to tire it. Even so, the animal often escapes.

Vultures crowd a silver-backed jackal as they flock to a kill in Africa (below). Vultures are scavengers. They feed on animals that die or on those that predators have killed. Vultures soar high above the ground. When one sees signs of a meal, it circles downward to get a better look. Its movements alert other vultures to the location. Jackals, although skilled hunters, also scavenge for some of their food.

Out of reach of hyenas and hidden from vultures, a leopard prepares to eat in a tree (above). It will return for leftovers.

a kill, these animals eat hungrily. A wolf can gobble 20 pounds (9 kg)* of meat at one time. A tiger or a lion can eat 60 pounds (27 kg)—three times that much.

Leftovers do not go to waste. Leopards hide their kills high in trees. Some predators, such as mountain lions, hide food under leaves and grass. The animals make several return trips to feed on the meat. One kill may last a mountain lion for almost a week.

*Metric figures in this book have been rounded off.

Because their food is difficult to obtain, predators must save their strength as well as their food. Most prey can outrun predators. Cats, such as tigers and leopards, creep as close to their prey as they can without being discovered.

These cats rely on surprise and ambush. They use their powerful front legs and sharp claws to pull an animal down. Then they deliver a killing bite. If the cats chase their prey before pouncing, they

do so only for short distances.

Many meat-eaters are scavengers. They save a lot of energy by feeding on dead animals. Scavengers scout the land for animal remains. Sometimes they steal meals from other animals.

Vultures are the most famous thieves in the animal world. But lions, leopards, and packs of hyenas will rob smaller predators of their kills, too. Small animals like jackals (Continued on page 18)

Set for dinner, a bald eagle perches atop a salmon (left). Like most animals, the eagle feeds on what it obtains most easily. It may fish for food, steal a meal from another bird, or eat dead fish and other animal remains.

JEFF FOOTT (LEFT)

FLIP NICKLIN (BELOW)

A California sea lion dives for its dinner (above). With its large eyes, the animal looks for fish, squids, or shellfish. In dark, cloudy waters, the sea lion feels for food with its whiskers. Paddling with its front flippers and steering with its hind ones, the sea lion can swim fast and make sharp turns. Such underwater moves help it catch food with ease.

FRITZ PÖLKING (ALL)

1. *Wings spread, a Eurasian kingfisher looks like a guided missile as it aims for its prey. As its name suggests, this bird fishes for food. When it sees a small fish swimming near the surface of the water, it makes a fast dive. Not every dive brings success, however. The bird may dive several times before making a catch. This kind of kingfisher is found in parts of Europe, Asia, and North Africa.*

2. *Traveling more than 45 miles an hour (72 km/h), the kingfisher hits the water. Its thick skull acts as a shock absorber.*

3. *Got it! Underwater, the kingfisher grabs the fish in its open bill. To swim back to the surface, it flaps its wings.*

4. *Shooting out of the water, the kingfisher displays its meal. The bird will fly to a tree, kill the fish with a hard blow, and swallow it whole. To make this series of photographs, a photographer set a fish-filled aquarium beside a pond where the birds fished. When the kingfishers dived for the bait, an automatic camera snapped the action.*

16

Caught in the grip of strong forelegs, a butterfly becomes a meal for a praying mantis (above). This kind of mantis, called a flower mantis, waits disguised for an unsuspecting victim. Its coloring, texture, and shape match the leaves and blossoms of its plant perch. The legs of a praying mantis look short when they are folded. When extended, however, they reach far to grab prey.

(*Continued from page 14*) snatch bites from the kills of animals bigger than themselves.

Hyenas, Cape hunting dogs, and wolves hunt in groups. When chasing a herd of animals, they usually single out a straggler. Then the pack works together to bring down its victim.

Animals that hunt in packs use speed, strength, and teamwork to catch their prey. Some other animals wait quietly for prey to come to them. Tricks or traps help these animals get their dinners.

Predators That Trick or Trap

The petals of a flower toss gently in the breeze. But one "petal" has two big eyes. It is an insect called a praying mantis that is waiting and watching for a bee or a butterfly to visit the blossom. The coloring of the mantis helps it blend in with the flower on which it rests.

The tree frog fools its victims in the same way. Its colors match the plants on which it lives. The frog's long, sticky tongue quickly grabs insects as they pass by.

By waiting for their prey to

18

An angler fish hides among tube sponges at the bottom of the sea (left). Its coloring and shape make the fish hard to spot. Angler is another word for fisher. That's what this angler is. It moves its fishing rod—a thin spine that sticks out above its mouth. A flap at the tip of the spine looks like a worm. Any fish that tries to make a meal of the "worm" becomes a meal itself.

A lunar landscape? No, these craters in the sand (below, left) were dug by the larvae of a small flying insect. The larvae, called ant lions, crawl round and round in the sand to shovel out circular pits with their flattop heads. Then they bury themselves at the bottoms of the pits. When an ant falls into a pit, the ant lion's long, sawtooth jaws pop out of the sand and grab the prey (below).

DAVID DOUBILET

HANS PFLETSCHINGER/PETER ARNOLD, INC. (BELOW, BOTH)

come close enough to catch, such creatures as the praying mantis and the tree frog waste little energy in obtaining food. Predators that play such waiting games try to station themselves in places where a lot of prey passes by. For instance, a garden spider places its web in the flight path of insects, such as moths and flies. If the spider fails to catch anything, it spins a new web in a different spot.

Other hunters do not rely so much on chance. These predators lure their victims within reach. The angler fish waves a thin spine above its mouth. The spine resembles a fishing rod. At the tip is a flap that dangles like a worm. When a hungry fish inspects the bait, the angler fish sucks the fish into its huge mouth.

The bola spider tricks male moths that are searching for mates. To attract them, the spider produces a scent like that made by a female moth. Then the spider sets about some sticky business. As a moth comes near, the spider swings its bola—a bead of glue at the end of a silk line. Zap! The glue sticks to the moth's wing or body. The (Continued on page 23)

19

Before a butterfly can escape, a
golden garden spider ties it up in
silk threads (below). The spider
waits until it has trapped
several such victims in its web.
Then it feasts on all of them
at the same meal.

Ready and waiting, a garden
spider sits at the center of its web
(right). By feeling the vibrations
in the web, this hunter knows
when an insect is in the trap.
To reach its prey, the spider
rushes along the spokes of the
wheel-shaped web. Wind, rain,
and struggling insects damage
the trap. Every night, the spider
patches it or spins a new one.

Hanging upside down, an Australian ogre-faced spider holds a sticky net close to the ground (right). When an ant passes under the net, the spider will try to nab the ant.

A bola spider waits in the dark for a meal (below). The spider gets its name from its bola—the ball of glue at the end of a thread. To attract a kind of male moth, it gives off a scent like the one females of the same species produce. When a male flies in close (lower right), the spider captures it with the bola.

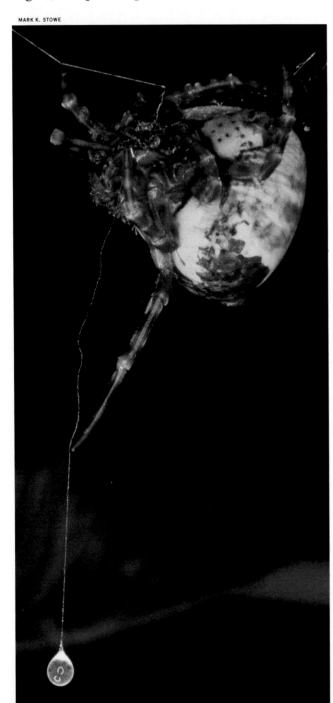

The drawings (below) show how the bola spider uses its unusual weapon. 1) The spider and its bola dangle from a silk line. The claw on a foreleg controls the bola thread. 2) At the buzz of approaching wings, the spider swings the bola. 3) The bola nears the target—a male moth that is attracted by the spider's scent. With the glue stuck firmly to the moth's body or wing, the spider will reel in its dinner.

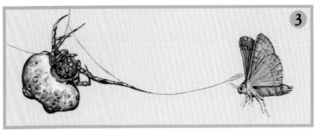

*Stretch! A common European tree frog wins the broad jump
—and earns a fly for a prize (left). The frog grabs its meal
with a flypaper tongue. Tree frogs do not eat during the
winter. They sleep in mud at the bottoms of ponds. During
the rest of the year, they feed mostly on insects.*

**Nose deep in dinner, a giant anteater feeds at
a termite mound in South America (below). Inside the
mound, the animal's long tongue rapidly shoots in and out of
termite tunnels. Each jab catches hundreds of termites on
the tongue's sticky surface. Anteaters eat ants the same way.**

(Continued from page 19) spider hauls in dinner. The bola spider fascinates those who see it in action. Other animals also have some odd—but successful—ways of obtaining food.

Some Unusual Feeders

The giant anteater raids anthills and termite mounds for food. It uses long claws to tear them open. Then the animal pokes its tube-like snout into holes it claws in the insects' homes. Its long, sticky tongue darts in and out of the narrow tunnels, catching hundreds of insects with each flick.

Many animals, including the anteater, must go searching for food. Some ants, however, have another way of obtaining food. These ants keep herds of tiny insects called aphids.

Sometimes, the ants carry the aphids from one feeding area to another. To eat, the aphids suck liquids from the leaves and stems of plants. The aphids, in turn, produce food for the ants—a sweet liquid known as honeydew.

Sea animals called cleaner fish and cleaner shrimps earn free meals by providing a service. These creatures feed on tiny animals and plants that live on the

Floating on its back off the coast of California, a sea otter uses its chest as a table (left). To open a clam shell, the animal bangs it against a rock on its chest.

A moray eel lets a cleaner shrimp rid it of tiny animal and plant pests (right). Cleaner shrimps feed on lice and plant growths. They also eat dead tissues. By cleaning wounds, they help the animal stay healthy.

A dairymaid ant guards a herd of tiny insects called aphids (above). The aphids are sucking juice from a plant stem. This kind of ant laps up a sweet liquid produced by the aphids. The photograph shows these creatures greatly enlarged.

skin of many fish. Cleaner fish and cleaner shrimps have bright colors and bold patterns that advertise their profession. Fish often swim from some distance away, then wait in line to be cleaned.

Some animals specialize in eating foods that other animals cannot eat. The shells of mussels, clams, and other kinds of shellfish prove too difficult for most animals to pry open. Both the herring gull and the sea otter have found ways around the problem. As the herring gull flies over rocks or other hard surfaces, it drops a shellfish from its beak. The fall breaks open the shell.

The sea otter floats on its back in the water and places a rock on its chest. It bangs a mussel or a clam against the rock until the shell opens.

Using a variety of methods, animals seek out and obtain many different foods. The energy supplied by these foods keeps the animals alive. It enables them to protect themselves, to find mates, and to raise their young.

2
Life at Stake

By Judith E. Rinard

Hiss! To frighten away a hungry dog or to look too big for a snake to swallow, this Australian frilled lizard uses a trick. Staring at the attacker, it opens its mouth wide and hisses as it puffs itself up with air. At the same time, it raises a big, colorful collar of skin. The quick display makes the animal appear big and dangerous.

Actually, the lizard only looks as if it might attack an enemy. It is acting, or bluffing. As soon as the enemy draws back, the lizard rises on its hind legs and runs away.

In the constant struggle to survive, animals use a great variety of defenses to keep themselves from being eaten. Some, like this lizard, try to fool their enemies — or to outrun them. Others have tough hides, shells, or spines to shield themselves from attack. Still others fight back, using powerful weapons to combat predators. Their aim in every case: to save their lives or the lives of their young.

On an open, grassy plain in Africa, a mother baboon rests with her baby. Other baboons feed nearby.

Suddenly, danger! A leopard moves quietly through the grass toward the mother and baby. The frightened female baboon screams a warning. In seconds, large males that belong to the same group, called a troop, rush to defend her. The males stand in a line and bare their long, daggerlike teeth.

The males begin to growl ferociously at the big cat. But the leopard is hungry. It will try to spring past the males and snatch up the baby. *Pounce.* The leopard moves . . . too late.

The big baboons attack in a rage. They charge from every direction and sink their sharp fangs into the leopard, stabbing at it and tearing it viciously. The big cat roars with pain and fury. Then, wounded and beaten, it snarls and slinks off.

Fight or Flight

Animals that hunt must kill other animals for food. Those that are being hunted must defend themselves and their young. Weapons—such as the sharp fangs of the baboons—help many animals fight off their enemies.

The defensive weapons of animals include sharp teeth, claws, horns, beaks, hooves, and even tails. With these weapons, animals bite, rip, gash, stun,

28

Jaws open wide, a male baboon displays long, pointed teeth (left). Baboons live in large groups in Africa. The powerful males protect the females and the young. Using their teeth, several males can injure an attacking enemy, such as a leopard, badly enough to kill it.

A three-banded armadillo of South America curls up (above, left). Soon it will be in a tight ball, protected by its armor. The nine-banded armadillo of the southern United States jumps when startled (above, right). Then it runs and digs into the ground.

scratch, peck, or kick. They may hurt, or even kill, an enemy.

Not all animals are as well equipped to fight off predators as male baboons are. Many animals rely primarily on another defense: speed. When danger threatens herd animals, such as deer and antelopes, they race for their lives. Their legs are built for running. Springing off the ground, they dash, gallop, or leap away fast enough to outdistance most hunters most of the time.

Portable Protection

Some animals cannot run swiftly or fight well. They have another way of protecting themselves. They wear suits of armor.

One such animal is the armadillo. Armadillos live in South America, in Central America, and in parts of the southern United States. These animals have hard, leathery plates that cover the tops of their bodies. In between the plates is flexible skin that allows

the animals to move and bend.

Armadillos range in size from 6 inches (15 cm) to 5 feet (152 cm) from nose to tail tip. Most kinds run for their burrows or dig quickly into the ground to hide when threatened. But the three-banded armadillo rolls itself into a tight ball. The armored plates of its body fit together as tightly as the pieces of a jigsaw puzzle. A cougar or other enemy cannot bite through the tough armor or pry open the tight ball.

Most fish really get the point when they try to flip over a spiny sea urchin to eat its soft underside. They get a painful jab in the mouth. The urchin (above, on the right) has long spines attached to a thin shell. The spines protect it from most enemies—but not from the triggerfish, on the left. This fish blows sand from under the urchin, tipping it over. Then the tough-skinned fish eats the urchin's exposed underside.

Who's there? A jawfish peeks out of its burrow in the ocean floor (above). This fish uses its big, wide jaws to dig a deep burrow. It lines the burrow with shells and stones. Most of the time, the jawfish hides inside or watches at the entrance for intruders or for fish to eat. If threatened, the jawfish backs inside the burrow, spitting out pebbles to block the entrance.

Underwater Dangers

Just as animals that live on land face a constant threat from predators, so do those that live in the sea. Many undersea animals, such as clams and oysters, have soft bodies enclosed in two hard shells. A hinge connects the shells. When the animals feed, they open their shells to catch tiny plants and animals that drift by. But when danger threatens—*snap!*—the shells close. Strong muscles keep the shells so tightly shut that few animals can open them.

Some sea animals wear a covering of sharp spines. The soft body of the sea urchin is protected by a dome-shaped shell. Needle-sharp spines stick out of the shell and grow as long as 6 inches (15 cm). If an enemy disturbs the sea urchin, the spines turn and point at the attacker. The moving spines warn the enemy to stay back.

Short spines cover the porcupine fish. When the animal is resting or feeding, the spines lie flat against its body. But when danger comes near, the fish puffs itself up into a ball by quickly swallowing air or water. Then the spines stick out like sharp thorns. A predator cannot bite or swallow the fish without injury.

Other sea animals defend themselves in different ways. Many avoid enemies by hiding among rocks or burrowing into the sand or the mud. Some fight back— through an unusual method.

The electric ray, the electric catfish, and the electric eel are all fish. The ray lives in seas, the eel and catfish in fresh water. These creatures have a shocking way of defending themselves: Their bodies produce electricity. The fish have special organs on their bodies that send out faint electric pulses to help them find and track prey. When attacked themselves, the fish deliver powerful electric shocks to jolt their enemies. The charge is strong enough to stun a grown person.

When a porcupine fish feels frightened—gulp!—it quickly swallows a lot of air or water and expands like a balloon. Then sharp spines that normally lie close to its body (left) stand out like a porcupine's quills (below). Few predators try to tackle this spiny ball. When danger passes, the porcupine fish slowly deflates itself. Then it swims off to find small shellfish to munch on.

Animals that live alone rely on themselves for defense. Animals that live in groups rely on others of their species to help them escape enemies or fight off attacks.

Safety in Numbers

Elephants, the largest of all land animals, protect their calves by living in herds. Powerful females lead these herds. When a lion or some other predator comes near a calf that has wandered off, the females move quickly around the calf. The herd's leading elephant raises her trunk. With an ear-splitting trumpeting sound, she warns the predator to stay away. If it comes any closer, she charges, pointing her sharp tusks at the attacker.

Many kinds of fish live in large groups called schools. The fish in a school may number in the millions—perhaps even in the billions. They swim together in close, precise formation.

If a predator approaches, the fish swim even more closely together. Like one large swimming animal, they turn, twist, dart, and dodge at the same time. The predator gobbles fish on the edges of the group, but those deep inside the school are safe.

Some animals use group defense in a very different way. They warn each other with community alarm systems. Suricates (SOOR-uh-kates), squirrel-size animals of southern Africa, use such an alarm

African elephants protect their young by circling them when danger threatens. Here, a female elephant stands ready to charge (left). She can trample a lion or other predator, or stab it with her tusks.

Slender suricates keep watch near their burrow in Africa (above, left). The tall animal is a lookout. If it spots a hawk or other enemy, it will give a shrill alarm cry. All the suricates will dive into the burrow for safety.

Fish called blue-line snappers swim in a large school off the coast of Hawaii (above). When threatened, the fish swim in a tight group. Those on the edges may be eaten, but those surrounded by others stay safe.

system. So do the slightly larger prairie dogs, a different kind of animal found in North America.

Both these kinds of animals come out of their tunnel homes to find food on dry, grassy plains. Hunting birds, such as hawks and eagles, easily spot the suricates and prairie dogs from the air. The small animals are also visible to enemies on the ground.

Suricates usually live in groups of about a dozen. Often they stay with ground squirrels in burrows

the squirrels have dug. Prairie dogs live in much larger communities, called towns. A prairie dog town may have several hundred members. The animals dig underground burrows with networks of connecting tunnels.

When the animals come out of their burrows to feed, some act as sentinels, or guards. They watch for danger as the other animals eat. When a sentinel spots a hawk or other enemy swooping down for a surprise attack, it sounds a

warning. Then every prairie dog or suricate in the community dives into its burrow. Through this combination of community warning and fast action, the animals help save each other from being caught and eaten.

Warning Colors and Chemical Warfare

Many animals that hunt, such as birds and lizards, rely on their eyesight to spot prey. To escape

33

Ready to strike, a California desert scorpion arches its stinger-tipped tail over its back (left). With a forward flick of the tail, it injects poison into a coyote or other predator. Though painful, the sting of this scorpion is not fatal to such an enemy. Scorpions use their stingers to attack prey—tiny lizards, insects, and spiders—as well as enemies.

To protect itself from ants, this Florida land snail (left) carries its own insect repellent. Although its shell protects the snail from many enemies, tiny ants can crawl inside the shell. They try to eat the snail's soft body. To defend itself, the snail oozes a bubbly, sticky foam. The foam is so thick that the ants cannot push through it. They go away and leave the snail alone.

Like a red stop sign, this leaf-eater grasshopper of South Africa warns its enemies with its color. The insect's body contains a poisonous fluid from the plants it eats. A bird that swallows the grasshopper may die.

the hunters, most small creatures run or hide.

But some creatures do not run or hide. They hop, crawl, or walk boldly. These animals wear vivid colors and striking patterns that carry a message: EAT ME AT YOUR OWN RISK. They have poison in their bodies.

Poison-arrow frogs, which live in the rain forests of Central and South America, come in a rainbow of colors and a variety of patterns. Many have bright bodies that

stand out like neon signs, warning other animals that attacking them may bring death.

The frogs produce a powerful poison in their skin. If a bird pecks at the skin or a lizard makes the mistake of taking a bite of one of the frogs, it becomes violently sick and often dies. Animals that survive this taste test learn to avoid poison-arrow frogs. The frogs' colors and designs remind the predators of the danger.

A few creatures use a very

different, but powerful, kind of chemical defense. They produce bad-smelling liquids or sprays to drive away enemies. The skunk is known for this kind of defense.

When attacked, a skunk sprays the enemy with a foul-smelling liquid from glands at the base of its tail. This liquid can burn an animal's nose, mouth, or eyes. It may even cause temporary blindness. The skunk can aim and shoot accurately at an enemy from as far away as 5 feet (1 ½ m). The skunk

Eye-catching colors and patterns make this poison-arrow frog (right) beautiful to look at. They also alert its enemies—mostly snakes and birds—to danger. The skin of the frogs produces a powerful poison. Some South American Indians wipe it on the tips of their blowgun darts to make deadly weapons. The frogs live in tropical parts of the Americas.

Meal or monster? From a bird's-eye view, this poisonous Hercules moth caterpillar (below) probably looks anything but tasty. It grows as long as 7 inches (18 cm) and as fat as a large cigar. Its striking colors and markings and its bristly spikes warn enemies to stay away. The spot on its tail may fool an enemy into seeing the tail as a head. An attack on the false head saves the real one.

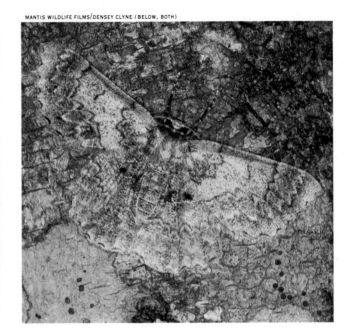

A white-tailed deer fawn lies motionless on the forest floor (left). Its speckled coat makes it hard to see. The white spots on the tan background look like patches of sunlight on the ground. By not moving even an eyelid, the fawn may escape detection by its enemies.

Now you see it, now you don't. The wings of a geometrid moth stand out clearly on a green leaf (above, left). When the moth rests on a tree trunk, its colors blend in so well that it seems to vanish (above). Hidden here, the moth may avoid being eaten by birds.

advertises its powerful weapon with black-and-white fur. Just the sight of the skunk's strikingly patterned body may cause experienced predators to back off.

Eye-fooling Colors

As you're wandering through a grassy field, you see a green grasshopper spring up suddenly and hop away. For a moment, your eyes follow its leap through the air. But when it lands in the grass, it seems to disappear.

Colors protect animals in different ways. While the skunk's bold stripes or spots warn its enemies to stay away, the coloring of the grasshopper helps it hide. This kind of coloring is known

as camouflage (KAM-uh-flazh). It helps keep many kinds of animals safe from predators.

Female ducks and other birds that nest on the ground often have streaked brown feathers to match the landscape. Their eggs have speckles and blotchy patterns that are hard to see in the nest.

Many creatures have colors that blend in with plants or trees. A green caterpillar sitting motionless on a green leaf is difficult for an enemy to see. So is a fuzzy yellow caterpillar resting on the petals of a yellow blossom.

Other insects have dull-colored bodies that blend in with the bark of trees. To hide, these insects must remain perfectly still. A bird looking for food probably will fly

right by them. The bird does not even notice the insects because of their camouflage.

Bluffs and Disguises

Some animals fool their predators not only with their colors but also with the shapes of their bodies. One insect—a kind of treehopper—has a pointed shape like that of a thorn. Certain other insects look like twigs or leaves on tree branches. These animals position their bodies to line up with real thorns, twigs, or leaves. Then the hunting animals often do not recognize them.

Not all animals come with their own camouflage. Some create it. These *(Continued on page 40)*

Peekaboo! On the ocean floor, a spider crab (below) hides by decorating itself with seaweed and plantlike animals. The parts of the crab's costume that look like white flowers are really live sea animals called anemones (*uh*-NEM-*uh*-nees). Suction disks on their bodies cling to the crab.

HOWARD HALL

A caterpillar called a looper, or inchworm, disguises itself as part of a flower (right). First, the looper bites off bits of the flower's petals and center parts. Then it ties them onto its body with silk threads that it spins from special glands in its body. After decorating itself, the looper moves about or rests on the flower—almost invisible to birds and spiders that prey on it.

JAMES H. ROBINSON (RIGHT)

38

During the day, an eyed silk moth of Costa Rica rests on a leaf (left). Its patterned wings blend with its background. They help hide the moth's fuzzy body from birds. If a bird should discover the moth and try to grab it, the insect spreads its wings. Flash! Two big false eyes appear (above). The eyespots may frighten the bird away. To the bird, they may look like the eyes of an enemy, such as an owl.*

(Continued from page 37) animals disguise themselves in costumes of sand, mud, chalk, plants, and plantlike animals. The decorator spider crab, for example, tears off pieces of seaweed. The crab chews the seaweed until it softens. Then the crab rubs the chewed-up bits across its head and legs. Tiny hairs trap the materials. For the rest of its disguise, the crab piles non-moving sea creatures on its shell.

Still other animals use bluffs to defend themselves. Bluffing is a way of playing a trick on the enemy. The animals do not plan the tricks, however. They do them instinctively—that is, they are born knowing how and when to bluff.

An animal that bluffs may try to frighten a predator by looking bigger and more terrifying than it really is. Many creatures inflate parts of their bodies or spread out

40

Trick or treat? A bird or a lizard that bothers this hawkmoth caterpillar (below) gets a scary surprise. The insect lifts its head high and inflates it. Two fake eyes bulge out. Suddenly, the caterpillar looks like a snake! This bluff scares some enemies away.

Resting all day on a leaf, a bola spider masquerades as a bird dropping (below). Few animals would want to eat it. The spider tucks in its legs and sits on a silk mat. It is unattractive and safe. This spider's unusual hunting technique is shown on page 21.

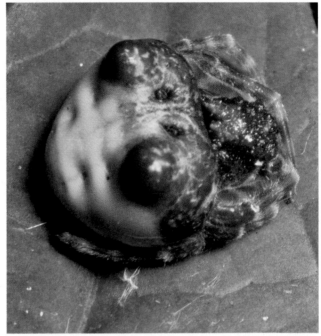

How many twigs do you see on this branch (right)? Be careful—one is an insect. The top "twig" is a looper, or inchworm caterpillar. To move along toward the leaves that it eats, it hunches and loops its body on the tree branches. If a bird approaches, the caterpillar stretches its body up at an angle and remains rigid and still. Most birds never notice it. When the danger has passed, the caterpillar hunches and loops off again.

41

An eastern coral snake (above, right) has a poisonous bite. Predators avoid its bright reddish, black, and yellow bands. The scarlet king snake (above, left) is harmless. But it looks so much like the coral snake that its colors protect it from enemies, too.

Which of these two (left) is the real wasp? The black-and-yellow hover fly, on the left, looks enough like the wasp, on the right, to fool most predators that fear the wasp's sting.

A monarch butterfly (right, bottom) that eats a certain plant becomes poisonous and tastes bad to birds. Birds avoid the monarch and its harmless look-alike, the viceroy, top.

their feathers or fur to look bigger. Others display scary markings on their bodies.

Many animal markings look like eyes. These false eyes, called eyespots, serve different purposes. Various kinds of butterflies and moths, for example, have false eyes on their wings. When these insects are resting, their wings are folded. If an enemy, such as a bird, approaches, the insect opens its wings and reveals the eyespots.

The eyespots may frighten the bird away, or they may confuse the bird into attacking the insect's wings. An attack on the wings would wound the insect, but it might spare its body—and its life.

A few animals look like other animals that predators fear and avoid. This resemblance is called mimicry. The viceroy butterfly, for example, has almost the same colors, pattern, and shape as the monarch butterfly. The bodies of

monarchs often contain poisons from a plant they eat. When birds eat monarchs, they may become sick and vomit. Afterward, they usually avoid eating monarchs.

The viceroy butterfly has no poison to protect it. But it looks so much like the monarch that birds stay away from it, too.

Animal defenses are as varied as the animals themselves, yet all defenses serve the same purpose. They help the animals survive.

42

=3=
Meeting, Mating, Minding the Young

By Sharon L. Barry

Side by side, a male and a female western grebe race across a marsh in Manitoba, in Canada. They arch their necks and hold their bodies high out of the water. The grebes splash noisily across the surface. Thrashing feet propel them forward.

The grebes' dash across the water, called rushing, is an example of animal courtship—activity that leads to mating. Rushing is the beginning of a complicated courtship ceremony. Western grebes perform this ceremony every spring during breeding season. It helps strengthen the ties between pairs. After the ceremony—and only after it—a male and a female grebe mate.

Not all animals have complicated courtship ceremonies like that of the western grebe. But nearly all have some kind of courtship.

Some animals take no part in raising their young. Others provide months or even years of care. Each species, however, does whatever is necessary for its survival.

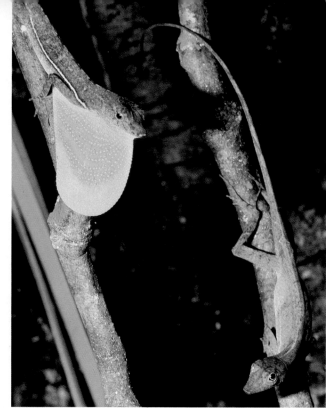

A male European bee eater presents a dragonfly to an open-mouthed female (above). This gift may help persuade the female to mate with the male.

Bobbing his head and extending a colorful fold of skin, a male anole lizard attracts a female in Costa Rica (above, right). His movements and colors help the female identify him.

In Australia, a male great gray bowerbird sits in the bower, or courtship structure, he built (right). Decorations he has collected will attract females.

Animals attract their mates in a variety of ways. During courtship, the animals may dance or strut. They may display bright colors or give off special scents. They may sing, bugle, or roar.

You might ask: Why all the fuss? The sights, sounds, and smells of courtship provide animals with important clues. These clues help the animals find mates of their own species.

Often animals must attract mates from a distance. Courtship clues ensure that the two sexes come together in the same place, at the proper season for breeding.

The right species of animal, the right sex, the right place, and the right time—that's what all the fuss is about.

Sights to Behold

Among most species of animals, males take the first courtship step. They invite females to mate. The females may or may not accept.

Some male animals use bright colors and flashy movements to attract females. Think of the peacock. He has a long train of bright blue-and-green feathers. To attract a female, called a peahen, the peacock spreads his train of feathers into a large fan. Then he parades in front of her. If the female is interested in mating with him, she pecks at the ground.

The great gray bowerbird is one of many species of bowerbirds. Bowerbirds are found only in Australia and New Guinea. Compared with the peacock, the male great gray bowerbird is plain looking. But he has his own way of attracting females. He builds a courtship structure, called a bower, out of twigs and grasses. Then he decorates it. He often uses flowers, fruits, pebbles, and shells. Sometimes he adds shiny

46

Two male elk battle in Yellowstone National Park. The stronger male will drive off the weaker one and win the opportunity to mate with females.

objects that he finds. A few other kinds of bowerbirds paint their bowers with the juices of berries. A female joins the male at the bower. There they mate.

Some fish and lizards put on colorful courtship displays. The belly of a male fish called a three-spined stickleback turns bright red when he is ready to breed. He swims in a zigzag pattern in front of the female. Then he leads her into a nest in the sand.

A group of small lizards called anoles (an-OH-lees or uh-NO-lees) have brightly colored flaps of skin, called dewlaps, under their chins. The male pulls his dewlap in and out. At the same time, he may bob his head rapidly up and down. Each species of anole bobs in a different pattern. Females respond only to the bobbing pattern of their species.

Courtship Battles

Sometimes male animals fight other males for the opportunity to mate with females. Usually the strongest males win these battles—and win the females. The losers rarely are hurt seriously.

Among animals that engage in courtship battles, the males often have horns, antlers, or other body parts that they use in fighting. The male elk has large, branched antlers. They measure up to 4 feet (1¼ m) across. Every year, in March, male elk shed their antlers. In May, new antlers begin to grow. The antlers reach their full size in late summer, just in time for the mating season.

The males announce the start of the season with loud, bugling calls. Then, as they struggle to

A male African lion rests in front of five females (above). They are members of the same group, called a pride. Generally, a pride has two to four males and many more females with their young. A female may mate with different males, and a male may mate with different females.

Young male giraffes spar, or play-fight, with one another (left). They do not hurt each other while sparring. However, they do practice a skill they may need when fully grown. Adult male giraffes sometimes fight each other over the right to mate with females.

take over groups of females, the males pair off. Pushing and shoving with their antlers, the two males fight until one gives up. The winner becomes master of a group of females, called a harem.

Frog Calls

If you have ever been near a pond on a spring or summer night, you may have heard the sounds of male frogs courting. *Peep-peep. Croak. Chirp.* These calls attract females and guide them to the ponds and streams where most frogs mate.

Different species of frogs usually breed in a single pond. Each species has its own call. The females can tell by the calls where to find the males of their species. One male may make a high-pitched trill. Another may grunt. There are calls that sound like clicks, whistles, bells, and barks.

Some male frogs have vocal sacs—stretchy flaps of skin—under their lower jaws. When a male calls, he fills the sac with air from his lungs. He forces the air back and forth from the sac to the lungs. As the air crosses the vocal

cords, they vibrate, making sounds. The vocal sac amplifies these sounds. If a group of males calls together, females can hear the noise from as far away as a third of a mile ($\frac{1}{2}$ km).

Spider and Insect Courtship

On a hot day, hundreds of kinds of insects may crawl, hop, and fly about a single field. One species may look very much like another. How do males and females of the same species find each other?

Sounds   *(Continued on page 52)*

49

A male barking tree frog calls from a pond in Florida (below). The frog pumps air from its lungs over its vocal cords into its mouth. The air is then pushed into a loose layer of skin, called a vocal sac, under its lower jaw. The sac blows up like a balloon and vibrates, making the sound louder. The call attracts females.

A chorus of colorful male golden toads sings at a small forest pool (right). Females, attracted by the calls, will join these males. After mating, the females will each lay hundreds of eggs and leave them. When the eggs hatch, the young will be on their own. Golden toads live only in a small part of Costa Rica. The males have a very different call from that of the tree frog above. Golden toads trill quietly.

50

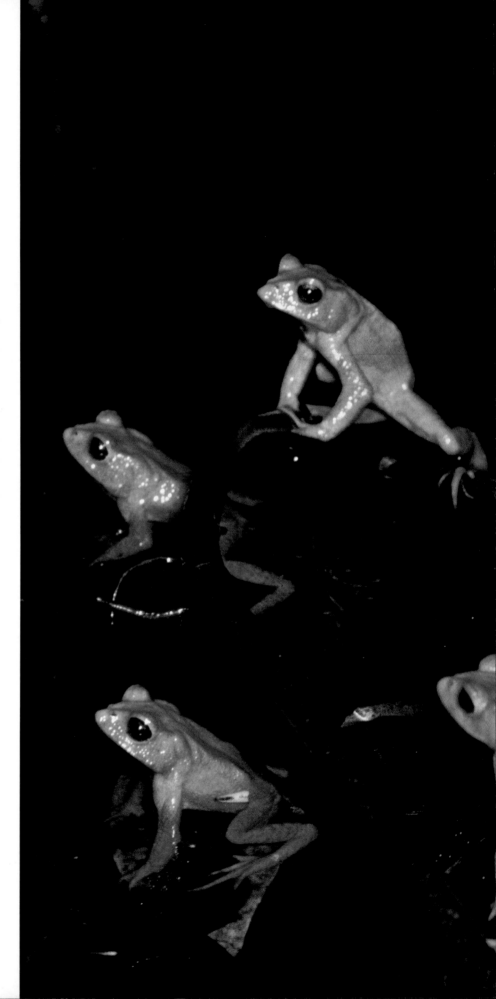

On a special mating thread, a female garden spider moves toward a male (above). The male, on the right, spins the thread and attaches it to the female's web. He plucks the thread to attract her. If he succeeds, she moves onto the thread to mate with him.

A female butterfly clings to a leaf with her mate below her (right). These butterflies, Burmese jezebels, live in Southeast Asia. Males and females have different coloring on the upper parts of their wings (hidden here). This coloring helps males recognize females.

(Continued from page 49) help some insects find mates. For example, grasshoppers "sing." They make sounds by rubbing their hind legs against their wings.

Other insects, such as fireflies, send sight signals. Each species of firefly blinks its lights in a different rhythm to attract mates.

Spider courtship can be a matter of life or death. Males are nearly always smaller than females. Sometimes females view males as prey and eat them. Some male spiders court females by waving their legs while at a safe distance. Others vibrate the females' webs. They do not try to mate unless the females give go-ahead signals. Still other male spiders present the females with gifts, such as flies. While a female eats the gift, the male mates with her.

Male butterflies often identify females by the way they fly. Bright colors and patterns also help some kinds of male butterflies find females.

Moths that are active at night don't depend on sight to find one another. They use scents. Males and females produce pheromones (FER-uh-mones), chemicals that have certain odors. During courtship, a female gives off a pheromone. A male finds the female by detecting the odor of the pheromone with his antennae.

Parents and Their Young

If all goes well during courtship, mating occurs. In time, most females that have mated lay eggs or give birth to young.

Not all animal parents, however, take care of their young. Many young can feed and take care of

52

A baby giant water bug hatches from an egg on its father's back (above). Female giant water bugs lay eggs on the backs of males. The males care for the eggs until the young hatch. By rising to the surface, as this bug is doing, the males help the eggs get oxygen. Underwater, the males kick their hind legs to deliver fresh, oxygen-rich water to the eggs.

A female crab spider guards her cocoon, or egg case, as newly hatched spiderlings emerge (right). The cocoon, spun of silk by the female, protects the eggs.

themselves from the start. Some never see their parents. Most kinds of fish simply lay their eggs and swim away. When the young hatch, they are on their own.

Fish themselves as well as other animals eat fish eggs and young fish. To help ensure that some young survive, female fish lay large numbers of eggs—often hundreds of thousands at a time.

Pacific salmon, fish that spend most of their lives in the ocean, swim into rivers to lay eggs. Females use their tails to make hollows in the gravel on the river bottoms. They lay eggs in the hollows, and males fertilize them. Then the fish sweep gravel over

their eggs and die. The new generation will hatch later.

Female sea turtles drag their heavy bodies out of the water to dig nests on shore. They lay their eggs in deep holes, cover them with sand, and crawl back to sea.

Female spiders spin silk mats and lay eggs on them. Then they spin more silk and wrap it around the eggs. Some guard the eggs until they hatch. Then they leave.

Among some creatures, the male cares for the eggs. Male giant water bugs, for example, carry the eggs on their backs.

A few kinds of male frogs also carry eggs on parts of their bodies. The male European midwife

toad—actually, a kind of frog—wraps strings of eggs around its hind legs. The Darwin's frog of South America carries eggs in its vocal sac. Among these animals, though, the parents' job generally ends when the eggs hatch.

Bringing Up Birds

Adult birds, like many egg-laying animals, begin their duties as parents while the young are in the egg. After a female bird has laid her eggs, she or her mate sits on them. The adult's body heat causes the chicks to develop and the eggs to hatch. Keeping the eggs warm is called incubation.

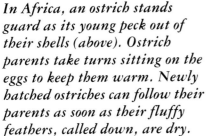

In Africa, an ostrich stands guard as its young peck out of their shells (above). Ostrich parents take turns sitting on the eggs to keep them warm. Newly hatched ostriches can follow their parents as soon as their fluffy feathers, called down, are dry.

Guarding the group, two adult Canada geese swim with several young in Alaska (above). Canada geese mate for life. Their young, called goslings, learn to follow the adults during the first days of life. A female Canada goose usually lays six or seven eggs at one time. These goslings probably belong to more than one set of parents. Sometimes families share the responsibilities of caring for goslings.

The young of some birds, such as pheasants or ducks and geese, can walk or swim well almost as soon as they hatch. Most ducklings, for example, leave the nest within a day. For the first few days, their parents help keep them warm at night. The adults also lead the ducklings to food and protect them from danger.

A special kind of learning, called imprinting, helps ducklings and some other active young birds to survive. During the first few hours after the chicks hatch, they become strongly attached to, or imprinted on, the first large moving thing they see. Usually, the first thing they see is their mother, so the young imprint on her. Then the babies follow her everywhere. By staying near her, the young are protected.

Most newly hatched birds are helpless. Baby robins and other songbirds, for example, cannot leave the nest. They depend completely on their parents. These young hatch either naked or with only a little down—fluffy feathers—on their bodies. Their eyes are closed, and they cannot walk or fly. Their parents feed them and keep them warm and safe.

Until their bodies are more developed, baby birds need help staying warm. At first, the chicks' body temperatures go up and down, depending on the temperature around them. To keep the young warm, parents take turns brooding—huddling over them. On hot, sunny days, parents may help the young cool off by spreading their wings to provide shade.

If another animal comes too close, the parents may try to chase away the intruder. Sometimes they distract an enemy by leaving the nest. They try to draw attention to themselves—and away from the nest and the chicks.

Young birds eat and eat and eat. A young robin may eat 14 feet (4¼ m) of worms in one day! Finding food to satisfy hungry babies keeps a *(Continued on page 59)*

55

1. *A female Nile crocodile in Africa scoops up her newly hatched young. The female digs a nest in a sandy bank and buries her eggs in it. For three months, she guards the eggs. She chases away or attacks animals that come too close. When the young are ready to hatch, they make croaking sounds inside the shells. When the female hears the sounds, she uncovers the eggs. Then, as the babies hatch, she carefully picks them up in her mouth.*

TONY POOLEY   JONATHAN S. BLAIR

2. *A baby Nile crocodile pokes its head out of its mother's mouth. Other young are probably lying in the pouchlike area at the bottom of her mouth. After the female has all the young safely in her mouth, she will carry them from the nest to the water. Female crocodiles usually provide the ferry service, but sometimes males do it. Adults may be 4,000 times as large as their newly hatched young. The adults have fine control of their jaw muscles and do not harm the young.*

③

3. The female releases her young in shallow water. The young will live in this protected area for several weeks or longer. The mother—and perhaps the father—will stay nearby. If one of the young runs into trouble, a parent will rush to help.

A mother chacma baboon nurses her infant. The infant still wears a temporary coat of black hair. An older youngster with a permanent olive brown coat, reaches toward the baby. When a baby baboon is about four months old, it begins to try a variety of foods. It may eat roots, berries, and seeds. It continues to drink milk from its mother, however, for several more months. A female chacma baboon may give birth to a new infant while she is still caring for an older youngster.

American black bear cubs curl up together in their den in Canada (above). The cubs are about two months old. They had no fur and could not see when they were born in midwinter. They will stay in the den with their mother until they are about four months old.

On Alaska's Pribilof Islands, fur seal pups crowd the rocky shore where they were born (right). In the top of the photograph are some adult females. They have returned from the sea to nurse their pups. Each will find her own pup by its calls and smell. Female fur seals nurse their pups for four months. After that, the young are on their own.

(Continued from page 55) bird parent coming and going. One kind of songbird may visit its nest as often as 60 times an hour to bring food to its young.

Under the care of its parents, a baby bird grows rapidly. After two weeks, a young robin weighs ten times as much as when it hatched. About the time a bird reaches adult size, stiff feathers replace its baby coat of soft, fuzzy down. Now the young bird is ready to learn to fly. Soon it will become independent.

Mammal Mothers

Mammals are animals that, as young, drink milk from their mothers' bodies. That is one major reason why young mammals couldn't survive in the wild without their mothers' care.

Unlike birds, most young mammals need to be fed and protected for longer than a few weeks. Mammal young may take months or even years to develop and become independent. Scientists classify you as a mammal, too. Think

about how long your parents have been taking care of you.

Mammal mothers may nurse and care for their young alone in a den or another sheltered spot, as bears do. They may raise the young in large, noisy groups, as seals do. They may nurse an infant and care for an older youngster at the same time, as monkeys do.

Some mothers help each other care for their young. Elephant mothers gather their calves together in groups called kindergartens. While one mother watches

A newborn springbok, a kind of antelope, struggles to its feet on the grasslands of Africa (above). Within an hour or two, it can follow its mother (left). It must be able to move with the herd to escape enemies.

High in the trees of a South American rain forest, a young three-toed sloth lies in a furry cradle (right). Clinging to its mother's stomach, it rides safely for about six months.

over the group, the others go off to feed.

Not all newborn mammals need so much care. Plant-eaters that live in the open, such as giraffes, zebras, and antelopes, are able to run soon after birth. When an antelope is born, its mother licks it and encourages it to get up. Within an hour or two, the newborn can stand and walk. In a few days, it can keep up with the herd. Because lions, hunting dogs, and other animals prey on antelopes, a young antelope's survival may depend on its being able to keep up with the herd.

Lions, bears, and many other mammals have young that are more helpless. Blind at birth, lion cubs can't walk well for about a month. Their mothers carry them, one at a time. A cub has a loose flap of skin at the back of its

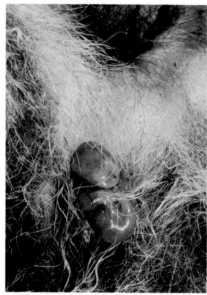

Blind and hairless, a newborn kangaroo, called a joey, climbs up to a pouch on its mother's belly (left). The tiny joey could fit in a teaspoon. Except for its mouth, nostrils, and front legs, its body is unformed. It uses its front legs to pull itself along.

Inside the pouch, a joey sucks milk from a nipple (left, bottom). After it crawls into the pouch, it attaches itself to the nipple. The nipple swells up, filling the joey's mouth. Much of a joey's development takes place in the pouch. The front legs of this joey now have claws, and its hind legs are forming.

An older joey pokes its head and front legs out of its mother's pouch (right). This joey, a red kangaroo, is about six months old. At eight months, it will leave the pouch for good.

neck. Its mother gently grasps this flap with her teeth, without hurting the cub.

Other mammal mothers carry their young in different ways. Three-toed sloths crawl upside-down along branches. The young ride on their mothers' bellies. A young monkey clings to its mother's fur and rides piggyback as she moves through the trees.

Babies in Pouches

The mammals called marsupials (mar-SOO-pea-uls) have a special place to carry the young. Most female marsupials have a pouch on their stomachs. Kangaroos, koalas, and opossums are all members of this mammal group.

Young marsupials are tiny and helpless. Their bodies have not yet fully developed. Kangaroos, for

example, are less than an inch (2½ cm) long at birth. They weigh less than an ounce (28 g). They have no hair, and most parts of their bodies are unformed. Right after birth, a young kangaroo, called a joey, crawls into its mother's pouch. There it stays, drinking milk and gradually developing. After about six months, the joey is ready to leave its mother's pouch for short periods. After about two more months, it leaves the pouch for good.

For the kangaroo, as well as for grazing animals like antelopes and deer, finding food usually is not difficult. They graze on grasses and other plants around them. Most young plant-eaters learn what to eat and where to find it by watching their parents.

For meat-eaters, though, hunting takes more time and effort.

In Canada, an adult red fox presents one of its young with a small animal to eat (below). When fox pups are about a month old, their parents start feeding them small pieces of meat. Later, they bring whole animals to the pups. This pup, about six months old, may not go off to live on its own for another six months.

A female lion stands guard as three cubs feed on a buffalo in Africa (above). These cubs are old enough to follow their mother on hunts. Watching her actions helps them prepare for later hunts of their own.

Pushing and yapping, young silver-backed jackals beg for food on an African plain (left). To feed the young, the adult will bring up food that it swallowed earlier. Jackals live in family groups. Older youngsters may help care for younger ones.

And for their young, hunting skills take a long time to learn.

Lessons in Survival

When lion cubs, for example, are a few months old, they begin to follow their mother or another adult on short hunts. They may be allowed to eat part of the kill. The cubs watch as the adult stalks and pounces on prey. The play of cubs resembles these actions. Cubs may stalk leaves and twigs and leap on them fiercely—as if the leaves and twigs were prey. At about 11 months of age, lion cubs start hunting small animals. After a few more months, the cubs are able to kill larger prey.

The parents of fox pups often bring small live animals back to the den area. The pups practice hunting skills by chasing and pouncing on the prey. After a few weeks of practice, the pups tag along with their parents on hunting trips. At six months of age, they are able to hunt on their own.

Wolves—relatives of foxes—hunt in packs. Their young have to learn group hunting techniques. When less than a year old, the pups travel with the pack on hunts. They help chase the prey, but the older wolves make the kills. Only when they are about two years old have the pups learned to hunt well.

65

4
Living Together and Apart

By Catherine O'Neill

After a meal, two young cheetahs groom each other. When these cheetahs grow up, they will live and hunt alone. Some animals, like the cheetah, generally live alone, except when raising young. Others live in pairs. Still others stay in large groups of family members. Some animals remain together in huge herds. Others live in crowded colonies where different individuals perform different tasks.

What helps keep all these social relationships alive? Communication. Animals communicate with one another whether they live alone or in groups. In a variety of ways, they exchange information about important matters—feeding, defending themselves, breeding, and raising their young. On the next pages, read more about the ways animals live together and communicate.

Feathery antennae help the male Polyphemus moth (above) find a mate. Moths normally live alone. At mating time, females give off an odor. Males smell the odor with their antennae and fly to the females.

Perched on a plant, a male Baird's sparrow throws back his head and sings (left). His message may be: "This is my *territory." Birds use songs for many different purposes. With its songs, a bird may give a warning, greet another bird, or court a mate.*

As a human being, you belong to a number of different groups. You're part of your family, of your class at school, and of your particular crowd of friends in the neighborhood. Within each of these groups, you have social relationships with other people.

In the natural world around you, animals have social relationships, too. If you observe your environment, you may find birds flocking. You may spot a mother cat fiercely defending her kittens. And you'll almost certainly share a picnic with a colony, or organized group, of ants.

When scientists observe animals, they look closely at the pattern of social relationships in a particular species. The scientists call this pattern social organization. Social organization can be as simple as a male and a female together at mating time. Or it can be as complicated as the cooperation of thousands of bees or ants in a huge colony.

Leopards are solitary animals— that is, they generally live alone. If you were suddenly to spot more than one leopard in the wild in Africa, you could be quite sure that you were looking at either a male and a female coming together to mate or a mother with her cubs.

The same would be true of other solitary animals, such as anteaters or koalas. Most animals spend much of their lives alone.

Some animals, however, live in large, organized groups. These include colonies of insects, troops of monkeys, and packs of wild dogs. Whether an animal is solitary or lives in a group, it has some sort of social organization.

Signs, Sounds, and Smells

To keep your own social relationships alive, you depend on language. At home, you talk over concerns with your family. At school, you discuss your lessons

M. P. KAHL

Snarl! *A male and a female leopard have a spat in the limbs of a tree in Africa (left). Leopards generally live alone, except at mating time or when they are raising young. During the breeding season, a female chooses a mate. After the young are born, the father may remain in the area for a while. He may help protect the cubs from adult males. Male leopards sometimes kill the cubs of other males.*

with your teachers and your classmates. With your friends, you tease and shout on the ball field, laugh at one another's jokes, and talk on the telephone.

Without spoken language like ours, animals must use other kinds of communication. They may use body signs. They may make sounds. They may communicate with odors. Some, such as apes, even communicate by means of the expressions on their faces.

You may have noticed that your pet dog makes a special gesture when it wants to play—a play bow. It stretches out its front legs and lowers the front of its body to the ground. Its hind legs remain

straight so the rear of its body sticks up.

In the wild, relatives of dogs, such as wolves, use play bows, too. A wolf that bows shows other wolves that it means no harm.

If a wolf or a dog faces another animal with its teeth bared and the hairs on its neck raised, however, it is sending an entirely different message. That one says, "Watch out!"

What other messages do animals send to one another? In the wild, they give warnings of the approach of enemies. A white-tailed deer, for example, snorts loudly when in danger. It raises tufts of hair over glands near its

hooves. At the same time, it gives off a strong odor. A wildebeest that spots an approaching lion snorts and holds its head high. Kangaroos give an alarm to others by thumping their hind legs on the ground.

Some animals help others of their species find food. Honeybees use a special dance to announce the location of flowers to the bees in their hive. Hyenas, animals that scavenge and hunt for food, make laughing sounds as they eat. The sounds may announce the location of the food to other hyenas.

Dolphins have been known to help one another in special ways. Although they live in the water,

GÜNTER ZIESLER

M. P. KAHL (OPPOSITE)

they are mammals. Like other mammals, they breathe air. If a dolphin is sick or injured, it gives a repeated whistle. Other dolphins in the area swim to the dolphin in distress. They push it to the surface so it can breathe. The helpers may stay with the sick or injured animal for days or weeks—until it recovers or dies.

Signs, sounds, and odors also help animals locate or avoid each other. Cheetahs usually live alone.

A cheetah that smells the body wastes of another cheetah will head in a different direction. But a cheetah's odor sometimes sends a different message. During the mating season, the smell helps a male and a female find each other.

Many kinds of birds use calls and songs to keep in touch with others of their species. Bird songs are more complicated than calls. A song may be made up of hundreds of sounds strung together in

a certain order. Usually, only the male of a species sings. With his song, a male might make his claim on a territory, or he might try to outdo other males. At mating time, certain songs help males attract females.

Animals that live alone as well as those that live in groups send and receive messages. By communicating in a variety of ways, animals help maintain the social organization of their species.

70

*Coated with pollen, a female honeybee called
a worker hovers near a flower (left). She visits
flowers to collect pollen and nectar for food.*

*Back at the hive, the worker performs a dance
as other workers gather around her (above).
Her dance—and the odors of the pollen and
nectar—tell the others where to find the
flowers she has just visited. Soon the
honeybees will fly out of the hive and head for
the food source. Even though they have never
seen the flowers before, they will fly to them.*

The Life of a Hive

Bzzzzzzz. Thousands of honeybees buzz in and around
their hive. Every honeybee colony has three kinds of
bees: a queen, drones, and workers. When a colony is
thriving, it has about 60,000 workers. The workers,
all female, have the most to do.

The workers build and maintain a honeycomb inside the hive. The honeycomb is made of cells the
workers make with wax they produce in their bodies.
Inside these cells, the queen lays eggs. She leaves the
care of the eggs to the workers. When the eggs hatch,
the workers care for the young, called larvae.

Male bees, the drones, live briefly. Their task is to
mate with new queens. The drones die as soon as they

73

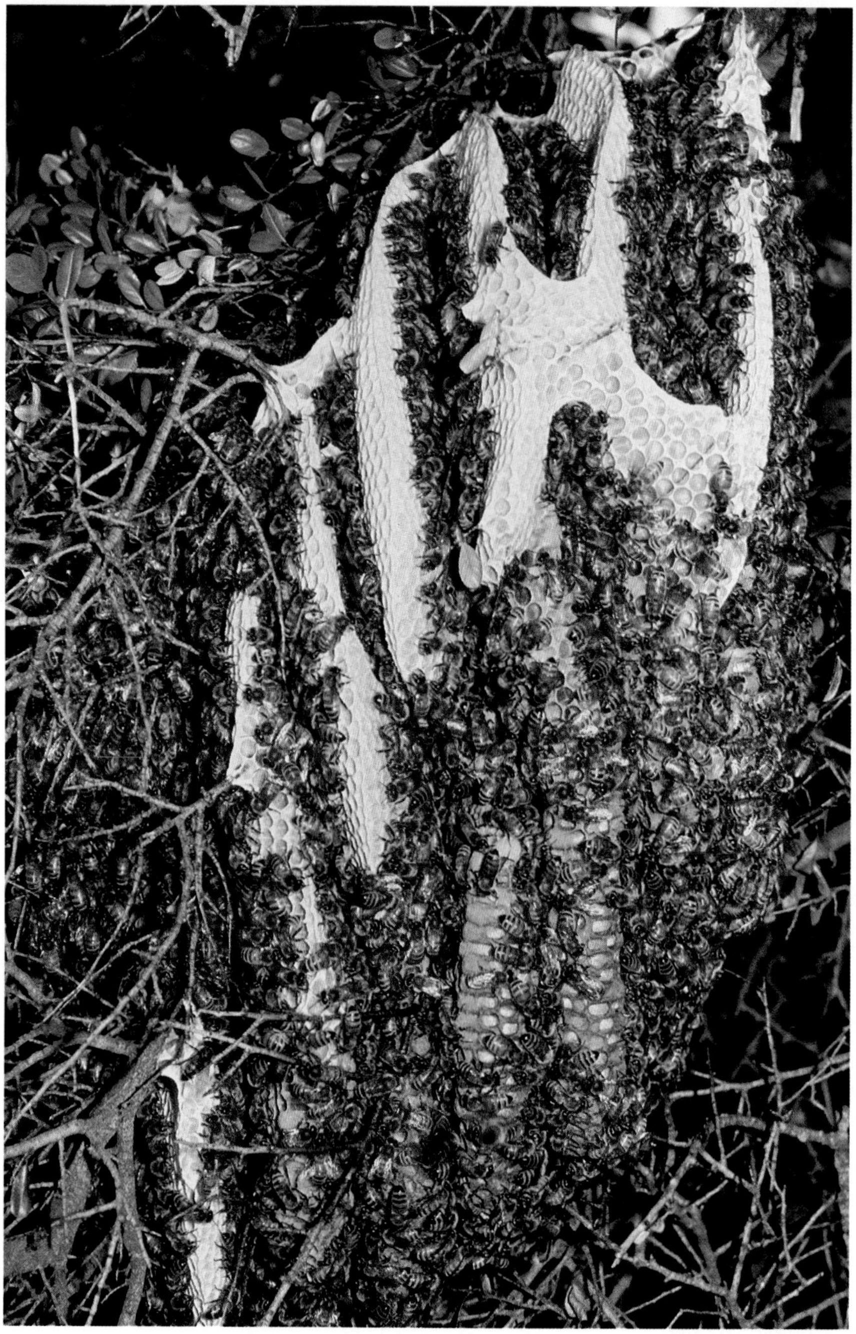

Honeybees buzz around their honeycomb (left). Workers build the comb out of wax they produce. Thousands of bees may live together in one colony.

Worker

Queen

Drone

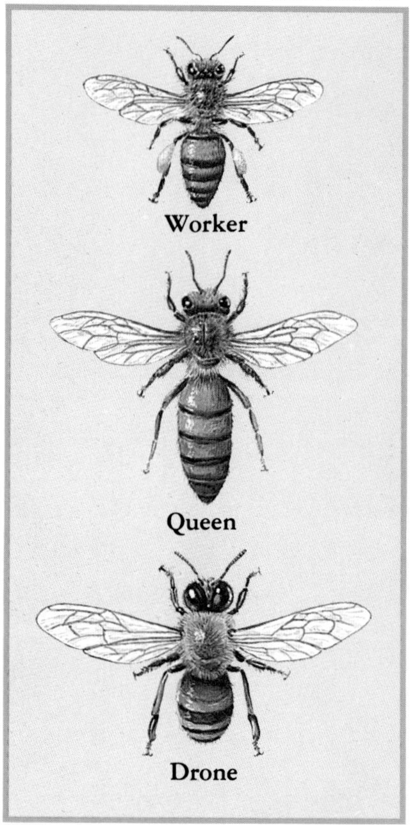

Among honeybees, different individuals (above) have different jobs. Workers, all females, gather pollen and nectar, make honey, and care for the young. The queen lays eggs. Males, called drones, mate with new queens, then die.

mate. The queens go off to start colonies of their own.

Workers provide food for the colony. They search for flowers rich in pollen and nectar. A worker that discovers such flowers returns to the hive and lets the other workers know about them.

In front of an audience of other workers, the returning bee performs a dance. If the food source is close, she performs the round dance. She runs in a circle, frequently reversing and going in the opposite direction.

The workers in the hive smell and taste the food the dancing bee has brought back. By seeking the same odor, they find the food.

If the food is far away, she uses the tail-wagging dance to tell the others the location of the food. She varies her movements to show how far away the flowers are and in which direction to find them. The other bees get the message from the movements and sound vibrations produced by the dancer in the dark hive.

Weaver ants form chains to pull the edges of a leaf together (below). This leaf will become part of their nest. Weaver ants build nests in trees. They make connecting tunnels and chambers from green leaves they have woven together with sticky silk threads.

Leafy home. Weaver ants scurry across part of their nest (below). The ant larvae produce the silk that holds the leaves together. To weave, adults move the larvae back and forth between the edges of the leaves. The adults signal the larvae to produce the silk.

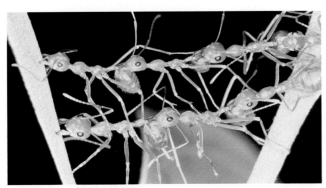

A bridge of army ants spans a gap (above). The ants have linked their legs and hooked their claws together. These ants frequently move to new nest sites, marching like an army. If they come to an open space, some make a bridge for the others to cross.

Ant Organization

You see them everywhere. They stream across a sidewalk toward a dropped ice-cream cone, invade a kitchen cupboard, climb up and down a tree trunk near your favorite picnic spot.

Ants searching for food are a familiar sight. More than 12,000 species of ants exist in the world. Like bees, they live in well-organized colonies. Within their colonies, ants share many similarities with bees. An ant colony, like a bee colony, is really an overgrown family. All the members have the same mother—the queen. Male ants mate with new queens.

Worker ants—all females—perform all other tasks.

In adapting to their environments, different species of ants have developed a variety of life-styles. Many ants make aboveground nests. Weaver ants live in waterproof nests made from leaves. Army ants link their bodies together, joined by their hooked legs. They form a living nest that protects the queen and larvae. Most other species of ants live underground. They build complicated networks of tunnels. Wherever a colony of ants lives, the members depend on cooperation to stay alive.

The young of a pair of Cape hunting dogs wait eagerly for food. Their mother, foreground, will bring up partly digested meat for them. She is the dominant, or leading, female in the pack. Usually only the dominant female has pups. She mates with the dominant male. Other adults in the pack help feed and raise her young.

Wild Dog Ways

On the hot plains of Africa live large herds of different kinds of hoofed animals: wildebeests, zebras, gazelles, and others. Here, lions stalk, and hyenas scavenge. And a lightweight, scruffy-looking animal, the Cape hunting dog, roams.

Cape hunting dogs are wild relatives of domestic dogs—those bred and raised by human beings. The wild dogs live and hunt in packs of up to 20 animals.

A Cape hunting dog pack is a tightly organized group. Most packs have several adult males, including a dominant male—the leader. However, a pack usually has only one adult female. When female pups grow up, they leave their parent packs. Several females from the same litter often form a temporary pack. These females search for males that have also left their packs.

Often the males and females join, forming a new pack. A dominant female soon emerges, and she

Hello, there. Two Cape hunting dogs greet by lapping at each other's mouths (left). Mouth lapping is a grown-up version of something these dogs did when they were pups. Then they excitedly lapped and nipped at the mouths of adults to beg for food. Adult dogs mouth-lap when they meet or before a hunt. Mouth lapping helps maintain the ties that keep the pack together. Because the dogs hunt as a pack, they depend on communication to bring down prey.

Okay, you win. A Cape hunting dog lies on its back while another member of the pack stands over it (right). This behavior shows that each dog knows who is "boss." The dog lying on its back has given in to the other dog. This is called submissive behavior. Pet dogs often act the same way. By lying down, the submissive dog will probably avoid a fight with the stronger, dominant dog.

generally makes life in the pack difficult for the other females. Constant quarrels with the dominant female cause the other females to leave the pack. Sometimes these outcast females do not survive on their own.

Generally, in any pack, only the dominant male and the dominant female mate. The female gives birth to large litters of pups—often more than ten at a time. The pups are born in an underground den. For the first few weeks, their mother feeds them with milk from her body. During this time, other pack members bring food to the mother.

When the pups are about three and a half weeks old, they begin to leave the den. Now all the adult members of the pack share in bringing up the pups. When an enemy—a spotted hyena or, perhaps, a jackal—comes too close and threatens the pups, the adult dogs chase it away.

At the time the pups first leave the den, they start to beg for food from members of the pack. The adults bring up partly digested meat for the pups to eat. Sometimes a pack of Cape hunting dogs kills prey close to the den. The pups may then share in a meal at the site of the kill.

For a few months after the young are born, the pack stays in one area as the pups grow. When the pups are about three months old, the pack abandons the den. The pups then begin to travel with the adult hunting dogs in the pack.

Wildlife biologists George and Lory Frame, who made some of the pictures on these pages, study Cape hunting dogs. They have found that it takes the pups a long time to grow up. The young may remain in the parent pack for as long as two years. Most of the males stay permanently, spending their lives together.

As the pups are growing up, they play with leftovers of a kill—pieces of tough hide or bones. They

tease one another, inviting a game of chase or tug-of-war. Some scientists think that the pups' play is useful. Through their games, the pups strengthen their muscles and practice hunting skills. Soon they will need these skills as they begin to hunt with the pack.

As a pack, the dogs successfully capture prey much larger than themselves. Cape hunting dogs usually prey on hoofed animals, such as wildebeests or zebras, that live in herds. The dogs' success in the hunt depends on cooperation. One dog going out alone would not have much chance against such large prey.

Before a hunt, the members of the pack run about excitedly. They grin and make high, birdlike twitters. They also lap at one another's mouths.

This mouth-lapping gesture—part of the dogs' complicated greeting ceremony—began in puppyhood. At that time, it meant "Feed me." As adults, the wild dogs use the gesture in another way. When grown-up dogs mouth-lap, twitter, and grin, they mean "Let's go hunting!"

Group hunting involves several steps. First, the dogs pick out an animal to attack—usually one that is slower, smaller, or weaker than the others in the herd. Then the chase begins. The dogs can run about 30 miles an hour (48 km/h) for mile after mile.

As the dogs concentrate on a single animal, the rest of the herd scatters. The leading dog keeps at the prey's heels. The prey runs in a zigzag pattern, so several different dogs end up leading the chase. Eventually, the prey tires and slows down. The dogs move in to bring the animal down.

Once the hunters have made a kill, they share their food with others in the pack. Sick or injured dogs that cannot hunt are allowed to feed on the prey. But first, the hunters allow the next generation of hunters—the pups—to feed on the kill.

GEORGE W. FRAME

During a hunt, zebras flee from a pack of Cape hunting dogs (above). The dogs usually go after prey smaller than zebras, such as wildebeest calves. But these predators can use skills that enable them to catch prey many times their size.

Wildlife biologist Lory Frame sits on the hood of her vehicle (left). She surveys Africa's Serengeti Plain for signs of the Cape hunting dogs she and her husband study.

A saddle of silvery hair across the back of a male mountain gorilla shows that he is 12 years old or more. Only such males, called silverbacks, lead gorilla groups.

Gorilla Groups

Deep in the shadows of a mountainside forest in Africa, the air is filled with a low rumble. It is the noise of mountain gorillas feeding. When resting or eating, these large apes express their contentment with deep belching noises that sound like stomach rumbles.

Mountain gorillas generally live in groups of about ten members. They communicate with one another through a wide range of sounds as they roam the moist mountain forests of east-central Africa.

During the day, mountain gorillas eat roots, tree bark and pulp, and other plant foods. They also rest

and travel about. At night, they sleep in nests on the ground or in the trees.

Mountain gorillas are endangered. People have taken over much of their forest home for farming and for other uses. Poachers—illegal game hunters—sometimes kill them as well.

Since 1967, an American scientist named Dian Fossey has studied mountain gorillas. Through her studies, Dr. Fossey has found that the gorillas are shy and gentle. To be near them, she lives in a cabin in the mountain forest. She observes the gorillas during

80

A mother and her baby nuzzle near other gorillas (left). Gorilla young receive a lot of attention. A gorilla baby stays close to its mother for its first two years. It clings to her chest until it is about four months old. Later, it rides piggyback. At night, it shares her leafy nest. A gorilla group may have several youngsters. They often play together.

On their way to a new feeding area, gorillas walk through the forest to the water's edge (below). Together, they will cross the stream. One mother carries a baby on her back. The leader of the group, a silverback, follows behind her. The silverback provides protection and decides where to nest, where to feed, and when to move on.

Up and over. A young gorilla plays in a tree (left). Young gorillas spend much of their day playing. They climb trees, swing on branches, and wrestle with one another.

A silverback gorilla sits still for a grooming session as two fuzzy babies watch (right, top). Grooming helps keep the fur of gorillas clean and free of pests. It also strengthens the social ties among the animals.

Four mountain gorillas and one human sit together in the forest (right). The human is Dr. Dian Fossey, a scientist who has spent nearly 20 years living among and studying mountain gorillas in Africa. To be accepted by the gorillas, Dr. Fossey imitated some of their behavior. Her research has uncovered many details about how gorillas live. Read in the next chapter about the methods scientists use to study animal behavior.

BOB CAMPBELL (OPPOSITE)

PETER G. VEIT

the day. "So that my own presence does not affect the gorillas' behavior," Dr. Fossey says, "I act like a gorilla." She imitates the eating and grooming habits of the animals. She also copies many of their sounds.

Dr. Fossey has identified 16 separate sounds that gorillas use to communicate. She has found that the animals may make barking sounds when alarmed or curious. They sometimes chuckle while playing. Gorilla babies may cry at times.

A gorilla's loud roar may frighten away an intruder. The roar comes from the group leader—a silverback male. He is called a silverback because of the saddle-shaped band of silver-colored hair across his back, a sign of maturity.

The band of silvery hair does not appear on a male until he is about 12. A group may include two or three silverbacks, but only one is dominant. Often, the dominant animal is the largest. The gorillas that follow a silverback pay attention to his signals.

Adult females usually leave the group in which they were born. They may join another group or pair up with lone silverbacks to start new groups. Males sometimes leave a group to live alone for a time or to form their own groups. Females never live alone.

This arrangement has its advantages. Females with young can depend on the larger males to protect them and their young. Gorilla babies, like humans, take a long time to become independent. They aren't ready for life as adult members of the community until they are about ten years old. They need the support and protection of others until then—something that gorilla social organization provides.

83

$\overline{5}$
Asking Questions, Finding Answers

By Sharon L. Barry

In Alaska, a female grizzly bear has just snatched a salmon from the river swirling about her feet. Her three young lean forward watching. Something else may be happening in this picture, too. The young are probably having a fishing lesson.

By watching their mother fish, young bears may learn how to capture their own food. Why do scientists think this is so? Years of observing and studying animals have taught scientists how animals feed, defend themselves, attract mates, raise their young, communicate, and learn.

Sometimes scientists study animals by observing them in their natural homes. Sometimes they set up experiments to study animals in laboratories. Whatever method they use, scientists usually start out by raising questions. As they answer one question, a new one often arises. In this way—question by question, answer by answer—scientists are learning more about how animals behave.

In southern Chile, at the base of the Andes mountains, young male guanacos look up from grazing (above). Over the years, the number of guanacos had been decreasing. Without information about how the animals live, scientists could do little to help them.

On a rocky ledge, Dr. William L. Franklin uses an instrument called a spotting scope to observe guanacos from a distance (right). By learning about guanacos in their natural home, Dr. Franklin is helping wildlife managers protect these animals.

In the Land of the Guanaco

Millions of guanacos (gwuh-NAHK-ohs or wuh-NAHK-ohs) once roamed throughout areas of southern and western South America. Now only 550,000 to 600,000 remain. Over the years, people have killed them for food and for their hides. Sheep ranchers have fenced them out of areas where they once grazed.

Today, there is increasing concern about the future of these animals. But to protect them, scientists need information about their behavior. What do they eat? What kinds of groups do they live in?

To answer such questions, Dr. William L. Franklin, a scientist from Iowa State University, studied guanacos in southern Chile. "Doing research on animal behavior is like being a detective," says Dr. Franklin. "I pull bits of information about guanaco behavior together to form a complete picture."

Young male guanacos live together in herds. Other guanacos live in family groups that include a male, about six females, and their young. The animals graze on grasses and browse on trees and shrubs. Detail by detail, Dr. Franklin learned about the guanacos' way of life. Using this information, concerned people are beginning efforts to protect guanacos and increase their numbers.

86

Fifi, a chimpanzee, reacts to a playful gesture by Dr. Jane Goodall (left). Dr. Goodall had been trying to tickle Fifi's year-old brother, Flint. Here, Fifi is six years old. Dr. Goodall has studied chimpanzees in Africa since 1960. She stopped touching them when she realized her study would last a long time. She did not want to interfere with their behavior.

Flo, the mother of Fifi and Flint, holds Flint (below). He was then only a few months old. Fifi, sitting at her mother's side, kisses Flint. Like all chimpanzees her age, she seems fascinated by infant chimpanzees.

Among the Wild Chimpanzees

In 1960, a young British woman went to East Africa to learn more about chimpanzees in their natural home. She expected to stay no more than three years. Today, Dr. Jane Goodall is still studying the same group of chimpanzees. Her study is the longest one ever made of wild animals in their natural home.

Why would a scientist spend so many years observing the same group of animals? "Chimpanzees are fascinating animals with well-developed brains," says Dr. Goodall. "They are more like humans than any other living creatures. I felt that a long study was needed to understand their behavior."

When Dr. Goodall first tried to follow the chimps through their rugged mountain home, they fled. After about a year, however, they began to trust her and to allow her to come close. Observing how different each chimpanzee was from the others, she started giving names to the animals.

As her study continued, Dr. Goodall began to make important discoveries. One day, she saw a

An adult Fifi, here 25, cares for her own daughter, Fanni. Fifi has become a patient, playful, and affectionate mother, probably by watching her mother, Flo.

chimpanzee trim the edges from a stalk of grass. It poked the stalk into a termite mound. Then the chimp pulled out the stalk and ate the termites that were clinging to it. Why was the chimpanzee's behavior surprising? The chimp had made and used a tool. Scientists had thought only humans made tools.

Dr. Goodall noticed many ways in which chimpanzee behavior resembles that of humans. Chimpanzee mothers form close ties with their young and care for them for many years. The young learn from their mothers how to raise their own young. Chimpanzees communicate by sounds and gestures. They hold hands and kiss. They pat each other on the back. After being separated for a while, two chimps may hug.

Dr. Goodall made her latest major discovery just a few years ago. She learned that the usually gentle chimps sometimes engage in a kind of warfare. They brutally attack members of neighboring chimpanzee groups. "Who knows what startling developments the next ten years will bring?" she says.

Tuning In to How Bats Hunt

In Central and South America lives a group of bats that hunt frogs at night. A scientist from Wisconsin, Dr. Merlin D. Tuttle, wondered: How do the bats find the frogs? And how do the bats pick out non-poisonous frogs from poisonous ones?

To help answer the first question, Dr. Tuttle observed frog-eating bats as they hunted at night. He noticed that if the frogs were silent, the bats flew right by them. But when the frogs began calling, the bats swooped in for the kill. Then Dr. Tuttle performed several experiments. In one, he tested whether

frog-eating bats find their prey the way many other kinds of bats do. Many bats send out high-pitched beeps, which bounce off objects. By listening to the echoes, some of these bats can tell where prey is. Although frog-eating bats use these echoes to navigate, Dr. Tuttle found that they don't use them to locate their prey. The bats locate frogs by the frogs' calls.

To answer the second question, Dr. Tuttle tape-recorded calls made by poisonous and nonpoisonous frogs. He placed two speakers in a large outdoor cage containing a frog-eating bat. Then he turned on the

Four frog-eating bats race through the dark toward bait held by Dr. Merlin D. Tuttle (left). Dr. Tuttle is recording the sounds the bats are making. To learn how these bats find frogs to eat, he conducted several experiments. For the studies, Dr. Tuttle caught bats in the forest, kept them for a few days, then returned them to the wild.

With its wings spread wide, a frog-eating bat swoops down on its prey (right). Dr. Tuttle found that such bats locate frogs by listening to their calls.

In Dr. Tuttle's outdoor laboratory, the recorded call of a nonpoisonous frog attracts a frog-eating bat (right). A tape recorder plays the call. At the same time, another recorder is playing the call of a poisonous frog. Dr. Tuttle found that the bats responded to the calls of nonpoisonous frogs and ignored those of poisonous ones.

tapes. The bat flew only to the speaker that played calls made by nonpoisonous frogs. Dr. Tuttle repeated the experiment again and again until he was sure of the result: The bats could tell from the calls which frogs were safe to eat and which were not.

This system works well for the bats. It creates a problem for the frogs, though. Male frogs must call to attract mates. When they call, nonpoisonous frogs are in danger of being detected and eaten by bats.

How do the nonpoisonous frogs protect themselves? Dr. Tuttle conducted more observations and experiments to find out. He learned that many nonpoisonous frogs have simpler, shorter calls than poisonous ones. Some nonpoisonous frogs do not call steadily but pause between calls. The frogs sometimes call near a noisy place, such as a waterfall, that disguises the calls. When nonpoisonous frogs see the shape of a frog-eating bat overhead, they stop calling.

Dr. Tuttle's experiments answered his questions about how frog-eating bats obtain food. His work also led to another discovery: The behavior of the bats has affected the behavior of the frogs.

91

Upside down, a black-capped chickadee probes a pinecone with its beak (above). It may be storing food to eat later or removing food it has hidden.

In a laboratory experiment, a black-capped chickadee stores a seed in an artificial tree (above). The experiment will determine how a chickadee later finds its hiding places—whether by sight, by smell, or by memory.

Dr. David Sherry removes a stored seed (right). When the bird that hid the seed returned to this hole, Dr. Sherry knew that it had been guided by memory, not by the smell or by the sight of the seed.

Testing Memory in Birds

If you have a winter bird feeder, you may have noticed that some birds, such as black-capped chickadees and nuthatches, may not eat at it. Instead, they often pick up seeds, fly off, then return for more. When the birds fly off, they eat some of the seeds. They hide the other seeds—each time in a different place. In just one day, a black-capped chickadee may store food in more than a hundred separate places! The storage sites include tree bark, branches and twigs, curled-up leaves, moss, and snow.

The scattered hiding places make it hard for other animals to find and steal the chickadee's food. But how does the chickadee itself find the hiding places when it wants to eat the food? Does it search until it spots them all? Is it guided by its sense of smell? Does it remember where it hid the food?

Dr. David Sherry, a Canadian scientist, predicted that the chickadees use memory to find the storage places. To test this theory, he set up an experiment.

Dr. Sherry built six artificial trees in a room near his laboratory. Each tree had 12 numbered holes in which a bird could store food. Dr. Sherry set out a dish of sunflower seeds in the room. Then he released a black-capped chickadee into the room. During a 15-minute period, the bird picked up some of the seeds and hid them in holes in the artificial trees.

After the bird was taken from the room, Dr. Sherry recorded the hiding places and removed the seeds. The next day, he covered all the holes. Because all the holes were covered and empty, the bird could not be guided by the sight or smell of seeds.

Then Dr. Sherry released the bird into the room. Out of the 72 possible holes, would the bird go to the ones where it had hidden seeds the day before?

Yes—it did nearly every time. Dr. Sherry got the same results using other chickadees. The experiment showed that chickadees use memory to find the hidden seeds. This excellent memory, Dr. Sherry believes, helps chickadees and other birds survive the winter and provide food for their young in the spring.

Sniffing the air, a white rat sits in the hand of Dr. David S. Olton (left). Dr. Olton has studied how much rats can remember. He tests their memories by putting them through a series of mazes.

Follow the squiggly red line and you will trace the path one rat took through an eight-arm maze in Dr. Olton's laboratory (right). To make this picture, a photographer attached a small red light to the rat's back. The rat, now in the middle of the maze, ran up one arm and ate the food at the end. Then it returned to the middle and chose another arm. It did not go up the same arm twice. Dr. Olton concluded that the rat remembered where it had been.

The A-mazing Memory of Rats

Chickadees aren't the only animals that use memory to help them find food. Rats, for example, search for food in many different places. If they eat all the food in one place, they search elsewhere.

"I wondered how many places a rat could remember," says Dr. David S. Olton, a Maryland scientist. "Can it remember where it has been? And can it remember whether it has eaten all the food there, so it won't waste time going back?"

To find out, Dr. Olton set up a number of mazes in his laboratory. The mazes were made up of alleys that were specially designed for rats. Most of the mazes looked like wheels. In place of spokes, they had 4 to 17 arms reaching outward from the center. Doors separated each arm from the center. At the end of each arm lay a pellet of food.

Suzanne and Suzette Malveaux, 17-year-old twins who live in Columbia, Maryland, helped Dr. Olton conduct an experiment for two months. They placed rats in mazes and recorded what happened. "We put a rat in the middle of a maze and lifted all the doors," says Suzette. "The rat ran down one arm and ate the food at the end. Then it returned to the middle and selected another arm. We wanted to find out if the rat would choose a different arm each time. If it did, we knew that it must have remembered which arms it had already visited."

The rats almost never ran down the same arm twice. They could remember up to 15 of the arms. "I never thought rats were so bright," says Suzette.

Further experiments answered more questions about rats and their memories. Some experiments showed that rats used landmarks to identify arms. Other studies proved that rats remember for at least eight hours where they have been and whether they have eaten all the food in those places.

MATTHEW NEAL MCVAY (BOTH)

Suzette Malveaux, here 15, of Columbia, Maryland, watches a rat return down an arm of a maze (right). She and her twin sister, Suzanne, worked in Dr. Olton's laboratory.

Holding a long microphone and a tape recorder, Dr. Harold Gouzoules records screams made by rhesus monkeys on an island in the Caribbean Sea (above). Dr. Sarah Gouzoules takes notes on the monkeys' behavior.

The Gouzouleses play back their recordings in a laboratory (below). An instrument called a sound spectrograph draws a picture of each scream.

A rhesus monkey (above) threatens another monkey. The monkey that is threatened will scream. The Gouzouleses have identified five screams, each with a different meaning.

The Meaning of Screaming

Rhesus monkeys, like many kinds of monkeys, scream when they are upset or involved in a fight. What do these screams mean? Drs. Sarah and Harold Gouzoules, of New York State, tape-recorded the screams of rhesus monkeys on an island in the Caribbean Sea. The monkeys had been brought to the island for study. The couple learned from the tapes that the monkeys made five different kinds of screams. For example, the monkeys made the loudest, noisiest screams when dominant monkeys challenged them or when they were having a physical fight. The scientists played back tape recordings of all five kinds of screams to the monkeys. Then the Gouzouleses watched the monkeys' reactions. The couple concluded that each scream carried a different message. From the screams, the monkeys could tell what kind of opponent the screamer was facing and how serious the danger was.

Pointing to a hand puppet, Dr. Herbert Terrace makes a sign that means "teeth." Nim, a chimpanzee, makes the same sign. In an experiment designed by Dr. Terrace, Nim learned sign language. Dr. Terrace wanted Nim to learn language as a child does. He raised Nim with humans and dressed him in children's clothes. The clothes helped Nim learn the colors and the names of various articles of clothing.

Can a Chimp Make a Sentence?

Thirty years ago, few people would have believed that a chimpanzee could learn to communicate with humans. Chimpanzees cannot make the sounds necessary to speak. In the 1960s, however, scientists began to teach several chimpanzees to use a sign language created for deaf people.

Dr. Herbert Terrace, of New York State, wondered if a chimpanzee could put signs together to form a sentence. He adopted a baby chimpanzee and named him Nim. Dr. Terrace and others taught Nim sign language. When Nim was four months old, he made his first sign: "Drink." At about eighteen months, he was combining signs to make requests such as "tickle me." By the age of four, Nim could make 125 different signs. He could also string together up to 16 signs in a row.

At first, Dr. Terrace thought that Nim might be making simple sentences. But as he studied written reports and films of Nim's signs, he became doubtful. He noticed that when Nim responded to his teacher's questions, he often repeated signs that the teacher had just made. Maybe Nim was mainly imitating his teachers. Dr. Terrace wasn't sure how close Nim's signing came to human language. He concluded that more studies would be needed to determine whether chimpanzees can actually create sentences.

97

By pressing keys on a computer keyboard, a chimpanzee named Sherman asks another chimpanzee, Austin, for some cheese. Figures on the keys stand for words.

Chimpanzees and Computers

In Atlanta, Georgia, two male chimpanzees named Sherman and Austin learned to communicate with each other using a computer keyboard. Each key had a symbol on it. The symbol stood for a word. When one of the chimpanzees pressed a key, that symbol would light up.

Two scientists, Dr. Sue Savage-Rumbaugh and Dr. Duane Rumbaugh, trained Sherman and Austin to use this language of symbols. First, they taught the chimps how to identify different foods by pressing the keys. Then they gave Sherman and Austin tests. They wanted to make sure the chimpanzees understood what the symbols meant. Through the tests, they also encouraged the chimps to communicate with each other. Finally, the scientists put Sherman and Austin in separate rooms. Each chimpanzee had a computer, which he could use to communicate with the other. An open window connected the rooms.

The scientists gave food to Sherman as Austin watched through the window. Would Austin use his own keyboard to ask for one of the foods given to Sherman? He did. What's more, Sherman looked at Austin's lit-up keyboard and handed the requested kind of food through the window! Then the scientists reversed the experiment. Sherman used the keyboard to ask for the food, and Austin handed it to Sherman.

Offering a banana, Dr. Francine Patterson makes a sign meaning "fruit" (left). Koko, a female gorilla, punches the keys of a computer in response.

On Koko's tenth birthday, Dr. Patterson holds up a present (above). Koko makes two signs at the same time. Together, they mean: "Koko love."

Koko: A 'Talking' Gorilla

What do gorillas think about? That was one question Dr. Francine Patterson, of California, had in mind in 1972, the year she began teaching sign language to a year-old female gorilla named Koko.

Some scientists doubted a gorilla could learn human language. Although scientists had investigated the abilities of chimpanzees to learn a human language, no one had tried to teach a language to a gorilla before. But Koko used her first sign, "food," a month after her first language lesson. Today, she regularly uses about 450 signs.

Koko often combines several signs. Dr. Patterson thinks Koko uses them to express her thoughts and feelings. Koko tells Dr. Patterson that she is happy, sad, or angry.

Occasionally, Koko seems to tell lies to avoid being scolded. Dr. Patterson thinks Koko knows when she is misbehaving. Once the gorilla described herself as a "stubborn devil."

When Koko doesn't know a word, she sometimes invents a new name for something by combining signs. For example, she called a zebra a "white tiger." When asked the meaning of a word, she uses signs to explain her answer. She can even describe herself. When Dr. Patterson asked Koko if she were an animal or a person, Koko replied, "Fine animal gorilla."

In 1976, Dr. Patterson brought a young male gorilla, Michael, to live with Koko in her specially designed trailer. Michael learned sign language, too. Now the two gorillas sometimes communicate with each other by signs.

Dr. Patterson talks out loud as she signs. Gorillas, like chimpanzees, can't make the sounds necessary to speak. So Koko sometimes communicates by using her own "talking" computer instead of signs.

"When I began teaching Koko, I had no idea she would progress so far," says Dr. Patterson. But many questions remain to be answered about the language abilities of gorillas. "We still don't know how much gorillas can learn," says Dr. Patterson.

99

Unanswered Questions

Belly up, a huge humpback whale bursts out of the water. For a moment, it seems to hang in the air. Then the heavy animal lands with a big splash. The whale repeats this spectacular leap, known as a breach, over and over again. Do such breaches help whales get rid of pests attached to their skin? Do the breaches contain a message for other whales?

Scientists don't know. They have learned a great deal about how animals behave, but much remains to be learned. In Africa, elephants sometimes gather around the bodies of dead elephants. Often, the elephants pick up bones and tusks and carry them around. Scientists don't know what this behavior means.

They do know that, with the arrival of cold weather, many birds fly thousands of miles to warmer places. Some end up in the same spot year after year. How do the birds find their way? Scientists are not sure. Someday, people may discover the answers to these and other mysteries of animal behavior.

FLIP NICKLIN

Index

Additional Reading

Readers may want to check the *National Geographic Index* and the *WORLD Index* in a school or a public library for related articles. These companion volumes in the National Geographic Society's series of Books for World Explorers also contain related material: *Amazing Animals of the Sea; The Mysterious Undersea World; Secrets of Animal Survival; Wildlife Alert!;* and *Zoos Without Cages.* Readers may also want to refer to the National Geographic Society's two-volume *Book of Mammals,* and to the following books for young readers:

Black, Hallie, *Animal Cooperation: A Look at Sociobiology,* William Morrow & Co., Inc., 1981. Coerr, Eleanor B., *Jane Goodall,* The Putnam Publishing Group, 1976. Davidson, Margaret, *Wild Animal Families,* Hastings House Pubs., Inc., 1980. Dean, Anabel, *Animal Defenses,* Julian Messner, 1978. Freedman, Russell, *How Animals Defend Their Young,* E. P. Dutton, 1978; *Tooth and Claw: A Look at Animal Weapons,* Holiday House, Inc., 1980.

Heller, Ruth, *Animals Born Alive and Well,* The Putnam Publishing Group, 1982. Kohl, Judith and Herbert, *Pack, Band, and Colony: The World of Social Animals,* Farrar, Straus, & Giroux, Inc., 1983. McClung, Robert M., *Mysteries of Migration,* Garrard Publishing Co., 1983. Michel, Anna, *The Story of Nim: The Chimp Who Learned Language,* Alfred A. Knopf, Inc., 1980. Patent, Dorothy H., *How Insects Communicate,* Holiday House, Inc., 1975; *Hunters and the Hunted: Surviving in the Animal World,* Holiday House, Inc., 1981; *Spider Magic,* Holiday House, Inc., 1982. Prince, J. H., *How Animals Hunt,* Lodestar Books, 1980.

Selsam, Millicent E., *How Animals Live Together,* William Morrow & Co., Inc., 1979. Simon, Hilda, *Frogs and Toads of the World,* Harper & Row Pubs., Inc., 1975. Walter, Eugene J., Jr., *Why Animals Behave the Way They Do,* Charles Scribner's Sons, 1981. Whitlock, Ralph, *Animals on the Hunt,* Childrens Press, 1982. Zweifel, Frances, *Animal Baby-Sitters,* William Morrow & Co., Inc., 1981.

JEN AND DES BARTLETT

COVER: A mother lion gently carries her cub across a road in Africa. With her teeth, she grasps the cub at the back of its neck. The relaxed cub hangs with its legs drawn up. Female lions may move their cubs from one sheltered spot to another. They carry the cubs one at a time, often making several trips back and forth.

Consultants

Maxeen Biben, Laboratory of Comparative Ethology, National Institutes of Health; and Fiona Sunquist, *Chief Consultants*

Glenn O. Blough, LL.D., University of Maryland, *Educational Consultant*

Barbara J. Wood, Montgomery County (Maryland) Public Schools, *Reading Consultant*

Phyllis G. Sidorsky, National Cathedral School, *Consulting Librarian*

Nicholas J. Long, Ph.D., *Consulting Psychologist*

The Special Publications and School Services Division is grateful to the individuals and organizations listed here for their generous cooperation and assistance during the preparation of HOW ANIMALS BEHAVE: Durward L. Allen, Purdue University; Thomas E. Bowman, John M. Burns, Ronald Crombie, Ron Hodges, Ron McGinley, James Mead, Robert Robbins, Mark Roth, Victor Springer, George Watson, George Zug, Smithsonian Institution; Ralph Browning, Alfred Godin, U. S. Fish and Wildlife Service; William Brownlee, Texas Parks and Wildlife Department; Thomas C. Emmel, Kent Redford and Fred Thompson (Florida State Museum), University of Florida; Francis Fay, University of Alaska; Dian Fossey; George and Lory Frame, Utah State University; Oscar Franke, Texas Tech University; William L. Franklin, Iowa State University; Jane Goodall; Harold and Sarah Gouzoules, The Rockefeller University; Jane Jacobson, San Diego Zoo; Thomas A. Jenssen, Virginia Polytechnic Institute; Charles Jonkel, University of Montana; Austin Magill, National Marine Fisheries; Diana E. McMeekin, African Wildlife Foundation; S. J. McNaughton, Syracuse University; Donald Messerschmidt, University of Maryland; Gail Michner, University of Lethbridge; Gary Nuechterlein; David S. Olton, The Johns Hopkins University; Francine Patterson, Gorilla Foundation; David and Virginia Pratt; Carl W. Rettenmeyer, Museum of Natural History, University of Connecticut; Jon Rood, National Zoological Park; Mark Rosenthal, Lincoln Park Zoo; Edward Ross, California Academy of Sciences; Duane M. Rumbaugh, Georgia State University; Sue Savage-Rumbaugh, Yerkes Regional Primate Research Center, Emory University; David Sherry, University of Toronto; David Smith, Donald Weisman, U. S. Department of Agriculture; Louis Sorkin, American Museum of Natural History; Eleanor Storrs, Medical Research Institute, Florida Institute of Technology; Mark K. Stowe, Museum of Comparative Zoology, Harvard University; Herbert Terrace; Merlin D. Tuttle, Milwaukee Public Museum.

Composition for HOW ANIMALS BEHAVE by National Geographic's Photographic Services, Carl M. Shrader, Director; Lawrence F. Ludwig, Assistant Director; and by Composition Systems Inc., Falls Church, Virginia. Printed and bound by Holladay-Tyler Printing Corp., Rockville, Maryland. FAR-OUT FUN! supplement by McCollum Press, Inc., Rockville, Maryland. Film preparation by Catharine Cooke Studio, Inc., New York, New York. Color separations by the Lanman-Progressive Co., Washington, D. C.; Lincoln Graphics, Inc., Cherry Hill, New Jersey; and NEC, Inc., Nashville, Tennessee. CLASSROOM ACTIVITIES produced by Mazer Corp., Dayton, Ohio.

Library of Congress CIP Data
Main entry under title:
How animals behave.
    (Books for world explorers)
    Bibliography: p.
    Includes index.
    SUMMARY: Explains how different animals obtain their food, protect themselves, court a mate, care for their eggs and their young, and live together. Includes profiles of animal behaviorists and research methods they have used.
    1. Animal behavior—Juvenile literature. [1. Animals—Habits and behavior] I. National Geographic Society (U. S.) II. Series.
QL751.5.H69   1984   591.51   84-989
ISBN 0-87044-500-6 (regular edition)
ISBN 0-87044-505-7 (library edition)

HOW ANIMALS BEHAVE
A New Look at Wildlife

PUBLISHED BY
THE NATIONAL GEOGRAPHIC SOCIETY
WASHINGTON, D. C.

Gilbert M. Grosvenor, *President*
Melvin M. Payne, *Chairman of the Board*
Owen R. Anderson, *Executive Vice President*
Robert L. Breeden, *Vice President,
Publications and Educational Media*

PREPARED BY THE SPECIAL PUBLICATIONS
AND SCHOOL SERVICES DIVISION

Donald J. Crump, *Director*
Philip B. Silcott, *Associate Director*
William L. Allen, William R. Gray, *Assistant Directors*

STAFF FOR BOOKS FOR WORLD EXPLORERS
Ralph Gray, *Editor*
Pat Robbins, *Managing Editor*
Ursula Perrin Vosseler, *Art Director*

STAFF FOR *HOW ANIMALS BEHAVE*
Jane R. McGoldrick, *Managing Editor*
Veronica J. Morrison, *Picture Editor*
Viviane Y. Silverman, *Designer*
Catherine D. Hughes, Tee Loftin, *Researchers*
Joan Hurst, *Editorial Assistant*
Artemis S. Lampathakis, *Illustrations Assistant*
Janet A. Dustin, *Art Secretary*

STAFF FOR *FAR-OUT FUN!*: Patricia N. Holland, *Project Editor;* Pat Robbins, *Text Editor;* Tee Loftin, *Researcher;* Ursula Perrin Vosseler, *Designer;* Roz Schanzer, *Artist*

ENGRAVING, PRINTING, AND PRODUCT MANUFACTURE
Robert W. Messer, *Manager;* George V. White, *Production Manager;* Mary A. Bennett, *Production Project Manager;* Mark R. Dunlevy, David V. Showers, Gregory Storer, George J. Zeller, Jr., *Assistant Production Managers;* Julia F. Warner, *Production Staff Assistant*

STAFF ASSISTANTS: Nancy F. Berry, Pamela A. Black, Cricket Brazerol, Dianne T. Craven, Carol R. Curtis, Lori E. Davie, Mary Elizabeth Davis, Rosamund Garner, Victoria D. Garrett, Nancy J. Harvey, Katherine R. Leitch, Mary Evelyn McKinney, Cleo Petroff, Sheryl A. Prohovich, Nancy E. Simson, Virginia A. Williams

MARKET RESEARCH: Mark W. Brown, Joseph S. Fowler, Carrla L. Holmes, Meg McElligott Kieffer, Susan D. Snell, Barbara G. Steinwurtzel

INDEX: Charles M. Israel, Jr.